THE CATCH-22S OF INDIAN EDUCATION

ONKAR SINGH

ISBN 979-888546045-3

Dedicated to my parents

Contents

Contents

Contents

Preface

"Education is the most powerful weapon which you can use to change the world"- Nelson Mandela

Presently, India is the second most populous and the most fortunate nation to have a demographic dividend in the world. This positioning endows the country with the onerous responsibility of contributing to the best of its ability in creating a capable human resource that can be of use for the betterment of humanity and sustainability. The recent onslaught of Covid has completely smashed the pace in every walk of life including education and calls for a lot of changes to tackle such threats to civilization in the future.

Education is the backbone of society and a prominent agent of transformation. The key drivers of the education system namely its regulators and teachers perform the requisite processes and practices pertaining to the programmes, curriculum, teaching, learning, examination, and evaluation involved in it. At the same time, the Government delineates and overviews education policies and overall performance.

Ancient India had both formal and informal education systems that imparted indigenous education at home, in ashrams, pathshalas, chatuspadis, gurukuls, etc. through people in homes, villages, and religious places for imbibing children with knowledge and life skills. But the growth of formal education system consisting of schools, colleges, institutions, and universities for meeting current educational aspirations has put forth a series of challenges in maintaining its integrity, accountability, quality, and relevance. Despite having worthy contemporary education policies in the country since independence, the milestone of best quality of education is still a dream. The deficiency of teachers in terms of quantity and quality, teaching infrastructure, poor academic governance, malpractices inflicting education processes, discriminatory practices, future uncertainties with students, poor employability, etc. are constantly alarming all stakeholders for the resurrection of the whole education system. Opening up of the education offerings by the institutions from the public sector and private sector have unlocked various good and bad which also need holistic intervention by the concerned to ensure their effective role in educating the youth. On top of all, the meager financing of education causing its continuous debilitation necessitates immediate action for mobilizing financial resources for a flourishing education system.

Let us understand that every hardship faced by the education sector affects the young generations immediately and the rest of the community in due course of time. Therefore, it is inevitable for education regulators, the academic community, and government to work synergetically and do the needful to provide the best education with access and equity.

I am presenting a compilation of my views on diverse issues pertaining to education in India with the hope that readers will find them helpful in understanding and contemplating imperative corrections. I shall be extremely grateful to the readers of this book to receive their constructive criticism of issues, indicating errors, omissions, etc. for improvement in the future at my email: onkpar@rediffmail.com

Onkar Singh

December 19, 2021

Acknowledgements

This book is a compilation of opinions expressed by me on various facets of education during the recent past.

I express my gratitude to my family for extending all support in the completion of this work. I am thankful to the publishers of all digital platforms namely ifp.co.in, therise.co.in, and timesofindia.indiatimes.com for carrying my view on diverse subjects related to education from time to time.

Not but least, I acknowledge the criticism and reviews provided by the diverse readers on these pieces of opinion.

Onkar Singh

CHAPTER I

2020: A Year of Shambolic Education Burdening Learners

Last month of the year 2019 gifted the world with the novel Coronavirus, first identified in Wuhan city of China. Thus, the year 2020 started with the rapid spread of the dreaded virus and the world got engulfed in the pandemic very soon. The whole of humanity got affected by it and lost a lot of fellow beings since then. The absence of adequate knowledge about the mechanism of spreading of the virus panicked everyone. An unprecedented path of lockdown was traversed by scores of countries, leading to the confinement of billions of Homo Sapiens within their homes.

India too was subjected to lockdown in the last week of March 2020 and everything came to a screeching halt. The academic session 2019-20 was nearing completion with only a few months left to final examinations. The pending studies were contemplated to be completed through distance mode. However, there was hardly any preparedness to negotiate such unforeseen health emergencies. The entire education system, starting from pre-primary right up to higher education, got disarrayed and various options were explored, including the promotion of students without examination, holding online examination, or holding offline examination after the resumption of normalcy, and many more. Neither the student community nor the educational institutions were equipped for online education delivery. Nonetheless, somehow with the meager resources available at either end, the academic activities were completed for that academic session. Those students who got promoted to the next level still had the opportunity of managing the learning gaps on their own during the subsequent course of their studies, but those completing respective education programs had to exit with certain deficiencies, and thus, were hit hard.

It was the result of a poorly planned lockdown by the Indian Government that the COVID-19 cases kept surging dramatically without helping the economy and the educational sector of the country. Subsequently, the academic session 2020-21 too started with the campuses still being out of bounds to students due to the continuing threat of COVID infection and teaching activities envisaged being conducted in online mode. The online mode of education started in the current academic session with some preparedness for carrying out remote teaching to students. However, the students still reel under the acute digital divide and struggle to learn. Even after a lapse of so much time since the beginning of COVID-19 in India, the educational institutions are unable to function as before the enforcement of lockdown.

Therefore, it will not be unfair to say that the COVID-19 has affected students in two academic sessions consecutively. Unquestionably the education system and regulators have tried and are also trying to ensure that the teaching-learning activities continue, but the extent of learning by the students in such a situation is likely to be deficient. The continued fear of the virus is not allowing students to return to campuses, meaning thereby that the student assessment and examinations are also being held in a somewhat similar fashion. in fact, there is great concern about the sanctity of the examinations being conducted in the online mode, in spite of the enforcement of the much talked about proctored examinations from homes.

Students have ample inputs to claim that the online examinations in regular courses are not sacrosanct and cannot be compared with the pen-paper mode of examination on premises of the respective institution. Even the teachers are aware of the challenges faced in the online mode of assessment and evaluation. Now, with the results also being prepared on fallacious online examinations, this may lead to loss of integrity of these assessments and create an adverse impact on the meritorious & ethical students who did not resort to any unfair practices in these examinations. Academics should work out a suitable action plan in the new normal to hold on-campus classes, either partly or fully, followed by the conventional mode of student evaluation so that the student credentials do not lose their integrity.

It is an opportune time to strategize for overcoming the deficiencies of the online mode of teaching-learning-evaluation processes. Some of the generic issues emanating out of the prevailing model of education due to the limitations imposed by pandemic are;

- Insufficient interaction between teacher and students;
- Limitations of online interaction due to varying socio-economic conditions and the digital divide;
- Inability to completely understand the content delivered online for theoretical and laboratory courses;
- Learning gaps due to unavailability of peer interactions;
- Poor sanctity of online examination system;
- Virtualization creating an adverse psychological impact on learners about the learning limitations;
- Uncertainty about future career prospects;

- Fear psychosis withdrawing the learners from marching ahead for on-campus teaching-learning, etc.

The academic community has to primarily brainstorm on all the issues pertaining to the learning gaps nucleated due to the prevailing 'Study from Home' option. At the same time, the learners should also ponder upon their learning deficiencies in the present setup, because it is the students who will take the brunt of their inadequate learnings in forthcoming competitive examinations.

Consequently, students are getting burdened with making up their learning deficiencies on their own. Students should take resolve for starting self-learning at the earliest and make use of the leisure time available to them. With the ubiquitous knowledge around as e-content and in digital form of learning resources, the students can overcome their deficiencies.

In addition, the regulatory framework of education should also enable the students to self-learning by providing access to e-content and knowledge resources that can be conveniently used for their improvement. The provisioning of the assessment tools that ensure the integrity of the evaluation process is also an urgent need.

****

CHAPTER II

Is upending teacher eligibility qualifications the panacea for higher education?

It has been made mandatory to hold a doctorate degree for entry-level teachers in higher education. Surely, the upgradation of eligibility qualifications is bound to add value to academics and appears a universal beacon of hope for improvement in the quality of higher education. But the factors challenging the quality of higher education need rudimentary introspection.

The worthiness of any educated one rolling out from higher education institutions (HEIs) is actually gauged from widely differing perspectives. For example, the research establishments look for sound fundamentals and understanding, the industry expects them to have the varying specific skill sets required by them, etc. Therefore, the purpose of education gets lost in the race for the livelihood of an individual and fulfilling the aspirations of employers and others.

However, the overall performances of HEIs are ranked by different ranking frameworks and act as an indicator of the health of HEIs for the public at large.

Indubitably, the teachers carry out the teaching-learning processes and the rigour of these processes ascertain the extent of competency generation in the educated ones. The capability and competency of teachers affect the quality of interactions with the learners. Nevertheless, the regular teaching processes in the classroom and laboratories are also a function of certain other enablers facilitating the teachers in these processes, so it is not the teacher alone who is solely responsible for the quality of education.

Dating back to the pre-independence and post-independence period, one can find that the number of doctorate degree holders were very few. The first PhD is claimed to be awarded in 1904 and since then the total number of PhD holders started increasing gradually. Till a few decades back, the sizeable number of senior teachers without a PhD degree could be located in India's HEIs. Surprisingly, this non-PhD. degree holders were also supervising PhD scholars and exemplary works have been carried out under their supervision. Thence, the PhD was not the binding qualification for teachers, and also, the quality of education did not get affected by it.

With the upsurge in the number of HEIs of University stature, the numbers of opportunities for pursuing PhD have increased significantly. Now PhD admissions are held regularly in HEIs very similar to the undergraduate and postgraduate admissions. The convocation statistics evince that there are certain HEIs conferring the number of PhD degrees in three digits every year. This upswing in the number of PhD degree holders is directly proportional to the aspirants. But the reasons for students pursuing Ph.D. degrees are not centred on their passion for research alone rather it is also the consequence of 'What to do after Graduation/Post graduation in the absence of any job?

It is very common to see that a large number of students continue studying i.e. graduation followed by post-graduation and doctoral programmes merely due to no other avenue available to them. At times, some HEIs seem worried about the quality of students aspiring for post-graduation and doctoral programmes. However, this concern takes a backseat when HEIs are made to compete with each other for better ranking whose process has these statistics too as part of some assessable attribute.

Ideally, the students in any course should essentially have a passion for pursuing it. It is also discomforting to see that irrespective of the subjects, a large number of PhD degree holders too are either unable to get employment or get underemployment.

There have been instances of substandard works being awarded PhD degrees by some Universities leading to their cancellation after establishing malpractices. The instances of plagiarism in PhD works led to the promulgation of specific regulations with punitive provisions for preventing it.

There are ample cases of inadequacy in the quality of research output in the form of publications, patents and knowledge creation as compared to the top-ranking HEIs of the world. Thus, core competence and the capability of candidates admitted in PhD programmes and the overall worthiness of a large number of PhD degrees being pursued in the country warrants an honest introspection by respective HEIs.

It could be understood from a simple case that anyone who is even below mediocre and devoid of passion for studying further, may move to pursue post-graduation and PhD degrees because of no other option available. In such case, the award of the PhD degree in due course may equip him/her in a narrow band of PhD related work, but the deficiencies in core competence, capabilities and skill sets may continue till one does not specifically work for overcoming them, which does not happen generally.

Thus, in the prevailing circumstances, counting on the PhD. degree as a quality assurance measure for the adequacy of knowledge and capability as a teacher does not augur well. There is the likelihood of some good postgraduates or even graduates who have been brilliant scholars in the primary, secondary and senior secondary level of education to possess better competence as a subject teacher at entry-level in HEIs.

Hooking up brilliant minds after graduation and nurturing them till PhD degree can yield better quality academics. Thorough brainstorming is inevitable for getting the best stuff as teachers in HEIs.

Why should not a framework be created for selecting the would-be teachers immediately after graduation based on rigorous testing on all dimensions required in a teacher and then pushing them for post-graduation and doctoral degrees at the cost of public exchequer in the form of scholarships for attracting the best minds in higher education?

It is the core capability of candidates that need to be assessed for choosing suitable teachers and mere dependence on some qualification may deprive the best ones of joining the noble academic profession.

****

CHAPTER III

How to reach the milestones set in the new education policy framework?

Education is the prerequisite for systemic transformations in society and the key operator for the sustainable development of present-day civilization. It is the man that causes happenings around. Therefore, the quality of human resources in terms of their knowledge up-gradation understanding, analytical capabilities, and skill development for contributing to society become critical. Unequivocally, the path to well-being and prosperity of any society treads through excellence in education with access and equity.

India's privilege of being the second most populous nation in the world entrusts it with the massive responsibility of ushering the world's humanity into a state of bliss. The education sector of the country being catered through primary, secondary, and higher education needs honest introspection. The policy frameworks have existed since 1968 and acted as the fountainhead of hope of excellence in education at all levels. Similarly, the recent National Education Policy 2020 (NEP 2020) is another such framework with ambitious provisions to achieve excellence in education. Doubtlessly, none of the education policies have ever erred in administering relevant frameworks suiting the contemporary requirements. But, the most sought-after excellence in education could not be achieved. However, the evidence of noteworthy improvement in the gross enrolment ratio at all levels necessitates an appreciation of the governance.

Among different focus areas of NEP 2020, the accordance of high priority to the achievement of foundational and literacy and numeracy to all students by grade 3 points towards the prevailing deficiencies of the mammoth education system of the country. Introspecting the detailed reasons for the plight of education in citizenry of the country, the weaknesses are apparently existing in the delivery systems i.e. in the education institutions.

All applaud to the NEP 2020 for being a 'light but tight' regulatory framework aiming to ensure integrity, transparency, and resource efficiency of the educational system through audit and public disclosure while encouraging innovation and out-of-the-box ideas through autonomy, good governance, and empowerment.

The moot point is how to reach the milestones set in the new education policy framework with the present setup having perceivable markers of inadequate infrastructure and human resources, questionable integrity, transparency, and resource efficiency along with various other limitations?

Brooding the downside of the country's education system signals numerous factors responsible for it which can be majorly bracketed into financial, administrative, and academic domains. Each of these is to be contemplated well for translating the impressive promises of the policy into reality. The disruptions caused by the Covid pandemic and the adaption of distance mode of learning using digital technologies by the whole of the education system in the hugely varying socio-economic society of India heralds new normal in which the preparedness for both on-campus and off-campus modes of education is desired.

The ruminations of the limitations creeping in the education system on account of insufficient financial support are evinced through inadequate infrastructure, human capital, and the absence of various other enablers. The desideratum of spending six percent of the GDP budget on education as envisaged by Dr. Kothari Commission in 1966 is an unfulfilled dream even to date. The statistics indicate that the spending of GDP on education has been hovering between 3-4 % since last decade. The proclaimed budgetary allocation on education in 2020 being at around Rs 99,000 crore sound noteworthy amount but with the vast population, the targeted aspiration of touching higher benchmarks of gross enrolment ratio, teacher-pupil ratio, bridging the digital divide, skilling, and overall access of good quality education to all interested citizens cannot be fulfilled with it.

With the Union budget 2021 in offing, the country's academics are eyeing appropriate budgetary allocations for education.

Especially, in the tough times of Covid disruption, when the educators managed the crisis of education delivery even by investing their own resources, the expectations are upbeat due to the lessons learned by the government regarding the infrastructure requirements.

The urgency for eliminating the digital divide, facilitating IT tools to those who are unable to afford them, strengthening of internet backbone, removing obsolescence, refurbishment of dilapidating infrastructure, creation of newer infrastructure facilities, recruitment of teachers, and supporting non-teachers staff along with other sector-specific requirements are the high priority expenditures entailing the adequate budgetary allocation.

The well-laid NEP 2020 has amply raised the aspirations of all stakeholders of education. The establishment of wide-ranging institutions for enabling the education system, upgrading of the institutions in terms of courses & subjects, upskilling of teaching and non-teaching human resource, creation of new institutions in the modified regulatory setup, etc. will ensue the compelling expenditures additionally in the upcoming year.

With the Prime Minister's trumpet call for self-reliance in the country, another indispensable component of expenditure emanates as that on research and innovation. The education system of the country nurturing the most fertile minds in their campuses hold the potential to contribute to solving the local problems through their research acumen while carrying forward the global aspirations of contemporary research and developments.

Though the country has already spent a lot on tackling the Covid menace and the freebies, the education system of the country has all legitimacy in expecting elaborate and impressive budgetary allocation for itself.

In view of education possessing the capability of being the panacea for the overall good of the society, the relevance of spending a larger sum on education does not call for any justifications and should be the driving force behind the forthcoming budget allocation on education in the coming year. Let us keep our fingers crossed and wish to see the higher percentage of GDP being spent on education that is in tune with the Kothari Commission recommendations of 1966.

****

CHAPTER IV

Another Sci-Tech Policy in the Offing!

Accolades to the makers of the Indian Constitution for envisioning the provisions to foster scientific temper in the country. Article 51A(h) of the Indian Constitution obligates for the development of scientific temper along with humanism, the spirit of inquiry, and reform as part of the fundamental duty of every citizen. This has pushed independent India to take up numerous initiatives in the form of policies in the field of science and technology.

The first policy related to science and technology was the Scientific Policy Resolution of 1958. It emphasized the creation of research infrastructure and basic research in all fields of science. Subsequently, came the Technology policy statement of 1983 aiming to achieve self-reliance and technological competence. Two decades later came another policy – the Science and Technology policy of 2003 – with a thrust on investing in research and development, finding solutions to the problems faced by the country, the most important being the creation of a National Innovation ecosystem. Ten years later, came a new policy, the Science, Technology, and Innovation (STI) Policy of 2013, with a focus on exploiting demographic dividends and accomplishing faster, sustainable, and inclusive development of the people.

Undoubtedly, the promotion of scientific temper and satiating the spirit of inquiry has been at the core of all policy frameworks. Tenets and beliefs with no justifiable basis have never been admired by any policy document in the country.

The Draft 5th National Science, Technology, and Innovation Policy

Kudos to the Government for reworking contemporary requirements and modifications to the existing policy framework and laying down the draft of the 5th National Science, Technology, and Innovation Policy (STIP) in the last month of the year 2020.

It is stimulating to see that the proposed Science, Technology, Innovation Policy aims to bring about profound changes through short-term, medium-term, and long-term mission mode projects by building a nurtured ecosystem that promotes research and innovation through individuals and organizations. The executive summary of the document speaks of its aim to foster, develop, and nurture a robust system for evidence and stakeholder-driven STI planning, information, evaluation, and policy research in India. The mandate is also given for identifying and addressing the strengths and weaknesses of the Indian STI ecosystem to catalyze the socio-economic development of the country and also make the Indian STI ecosystem globally competitive.

There is provision for an open centralized database platform for all financial schemes, programs, grants, and incentives existing in the ecosystem. Also, an all-encompassing Open Science Framework is to be created for providing access to scientific data, information, knowledge, and resources to everyone in the country and all those who are engaging with the Indian STI ecosystem on an equal partnership basis. The proposed availability of inputs and outputs from publicly-funded research to everyone under findable, accessible, interoperable, and reusable terms may boost the research activities through enhanced networking and mutual cooperation. The accessibility of journal articles and publications to all is likely to be there from a "One nation, One Subscription" policy.

The hybrid financing from centre and state is contemplated along with the requirement for each department/ ministry in the central, the state and the local governments, public sector enterprises, private sector companies, and startups to have STI unit with a minimum earmarked budget to pursue STI activities. The diversification and doubling of the share of extramural R&D support of the Central government agencies in the Gross Domestic Expenditure on R&D (GERD) in the next five years will necessarily revitalize the STI ecosystem.

It is enthusing to find the suitable amendment of General Financial Rules (GFR) for large scale mission mode programmes and projects of national importance to facilitate ease of doing research. Efficient disbursement, communication, monitoring, and time-bound evaluation mechanisms and audits are provided for supporting the conducive investment.

New Centres & Institutions proposed

Like other policy documents, the STIP also endorses numerous acronyms pertaining to various initiatives and new establishments. There is an indication of the establishment of Higher Education Research Centres (HERC) and Collaborative Research Centres (CRC) for providing research inputs to policymakers and bringing together stakeholders along with setting up of Teaching-Learning centres (TLCs) to upskill faculty members, which in turn will improve the quality of education.

The draft STIP looks upon the creation of proper protocols for aligning foundational research in India with the global standards while reorienting the research culture to recognize social impacts along with academic achievements.

The integration of Traditional Knowledge Systems (TKS) and grassroots innovation into the overall education, research, and innovation system is conceived through collaborations, fellowships, financing along with necessary support for fetching Intellectual Property Right (IPR) or any type of legal claim with the help of Higher Education Institute (HEIs).

Prime Minister's call for self-reliance ('Atmanirbharta') has found its place in STIP. It targets to align national priorities, like sustainability and social benefit, and resources. International engagements will be facilitated to gain essential know-how towards creation and development of indigenous technologies through Technology Support Framework and creation of Strategic Technology Board (STB) to link different strategic departments along with setting up of a Strategic Technology Development Fund (STDF) to incentivize the private sector and HEIs.

An India-centric Equity & Inclusion (E&I) charter is aimed at tackling all forms of discrimination, exclusions, and inequalities in STI for women, those from rural remote areas, marginalized communities, differently-abled individuals including Divyangjans, irrespective of their socio-economic backgrounds, proportionate representation of women in selection/ evaluation committees, addressing of ageism related issues and consideration of experienced women scientists for leadership roles and regular gender and social audits in academic and professional organizations.

The setting up of robust Research and Innovation (R&I) governance framework, STI collaboration framework for facilitating, stimulating, and coordinating R&D activities across the sectors along with the establishment of Capacity Building Authority to help plan, design, implement and monitor capacity-building programmes at the national and state level may accomplish better outcomes on the areas of national priorities.

Another institution, namely STI Policy Institute is proposed to be established to build and maintain a robust interoperable STI metadata architecture while promoting nationally and internationally relevant STI policy research and strengthening the science advice mechanism at national, sub-national, and international levels through training and fellowships.

Mainstreaming science communication, and public engagement through television, community radio, comics, popular science programmes, citizen media projects, science media centres, etc. is provisioned in STIP. The draft policy also calls for meaningful engagement with the Indian scientific diaspora for fetching the best talent back home through S&T for diplomacy and virtual international knowledge centres.

How effective would be the 5th STIP?

Apparently, the STIP seems to provide a well-crafted ambitious framework, but the challenge lies in its execution and capabilities to circumvent the operational limitations in the non-conducive socio-economic conditions. The reiteration of the country's STI requirements through a policy framework should stimulate the overall growth.

However, for matching the pace of global development, it is inevitable to bring the community out of the conservatism and overgrowing adherence to unscientific beliefs and dogmas, howsoever minuscule these numbers may be. The repeated instances of human killings on account of various tenets need stringent handling for enhancing the impact of science, technology, and innovation for the growth of society. The rising popularity of unscientific practices with many of them even being fuelled by government agencies and policies in different sectors may prove counter-productive to our endeavours to achieve the goals of Article 51A(h). The ongoing 'Save Healthcare India Movement' and the Indian Medical Association's (IMA) proposed relay hunger strike against 'mixopathy' "to restore the purity of the modern medical profession" is one of the best examples of the pushback from the scientific community against the government's notification allowing Ayurvedic doctors to perform complicated surgery such as excisions of benign tumours, amputation of gangrene, and nasal among others.

The proposed STIP would not be effective unless the quest for science and scientific temper is promoted by the government policies, authorities, and national leaders, including Ministers and the Prime Minister!

****

CHAPTER V

Rhetoric of common syllabus in universities may diminish possibility of achieving excellence

For quite some time, higher education regulators in certain states in the country are sanguine about ameliorating higher education through the common syllabus in respective state universities. There exists a well-laid out process of accreditation for assessing the quality of education imparted by higher education institutions (HEIs) through the National Assessment and Accreditation Council (NAAC) and the need for accreditation is also being cogently pushed through for quality benchmarking. But the pace at which HEIs are getting accredited bespeaks lackadaisical approach and the concerns for the quality of education imparted by them are not unfounded. Time and again, the discussions are abuzz for enforcing various measures for boosting the education quality and in turn enhancing the worthiness of educated ones graduating out, which is inevitable for exploiting the demographic dividend.

In general, the quality of education is termed as a function of faculty, curriculum, infrastructure, research activities, supporting staff, and facilitating administrative policies and practices. Consequently, the curriculum appears a discerning component for qualitative improvement. The courses detailed in the curriculum have their syllabus prescribing the goals, objectives, coverage, and its correlation with other courses. The syllabus delineates the extent of knowledge sharing with the learners and any deficiency in it is bound to yield deficient knowledge of learners. Therefore, the syllabus for every programme offered by HEIs should be of global standards.

Role of HEIs in syllabus making

Fortunately, the higher education of the country is imparted through Universities or deemed to be Universities which are autonomous. These institutions are amply empowered statutorily for devising the syllabus for the programmes offered by them. Accordingly, the HEIs ought to discharge the paramount responsibility of deciding the programmes and their syllabus.

A perusal of the process of syllabus making evinces the role of specific groups called the Board of Studies or some other resembling body entrusted with this job. These groups have the participation of all teachers of the respective department(s) offering the programme along with outside experts and representative stakeholders. Notwithstanding slight variations in the composition of these specific groups for syllabus making, the cardinal principle of participation of the teachers from the department running the programme is essentially there. Thereupon, the bigger statutory bodies accord the approvals on it, however, these bodies are devoid of experts from all subjects and may have competence for only ostensible overviewing. Thence, the onus of the content and standard of syllabus depends principally on such teachers.

In general, it is said that the HEIs do have a mechanism to take feedback from their alumni and employers about the quality of the programme in all aspects including the syllabus. If so, why the syllabus does not remain up to date despite all authority vested with the HEIs. Conspicuously, the downgrading of the syllabus of any programme in HEIs in India germinates from the inadequate rigour in the syllabus making process at the very first level which means that the teachers, external experts, alumni, employers, etc. do not perform the tasks holistically. If even after the comprehensive exercise behind the syllabus making, the standard of the syllabus is not met, the complacency in this task is to be viewed seriously. HEI leadership has to ensure the proper discharge of jobs assigned to respective groups in syllabus making so that the syllabus is framed as per the global requirements of the particular programme and not as per the whims and convenience of the concerned teachers.

Distinctiveness is opportunity

All HEIs by and large run similar programmes, but the worthiness of these programmes among the respective HEIs is hugely varying. However, due to identical programmes offered by a lot of HEIs, such programmes are blessed to purvey the distinctiveness from the forte of their faculty prowess. The aspiring students and employers view the programmes with similar degrees differently for different HEIs. Thus, the differing public perception about the programmes and HEIs mean that the statutory empowerment of HEIs to have their curriculum and teaching-learning processes seems to have been exercised with different degree of thoroughness. The stakeholders form an opinion about HEIs and their programmes based on the performance of the students passed out from them and the same depends upon various factors out of which syllabus is just one.

Undoubtedly, every HEI wishes to offer the best quality education for being distinctive from others to attract the best students to its campus. The syllabus of any programme happens to be its foundation stone as the content prescribed by it fixes the upper limit of knowledge transfer by the institution to students. Therefore, the HEIs should carry out the syllabus making process with utmost care so that the very first opportunity to nucleate distinctiveness in the programme(s) offered by it is harnessed effectively.

Usually, the syllabus for similar programmes is quite identical with a few variations in them. In such a situation every HEI must focus on creating a curriculum that leads to the excellence of the whole programme with a focus on the specialities with them. It goes without saying that the other factors of teaching-learning processes are to be taken care of appropriately. Common syllabus regulation could be a trap for generalization of education and at the end, the HEIs may find it difficult to excel in some niche areas depending upon their focus. However, certain minimum standards as prescribed by the national education regulators should be adhered to for each programme by all HEIs and these be exhorted to have their distinctive syllabus. A cue can be had from the Institutions of national importance where the uniqueness of syllabus for the programmes has created specific perceptions depending upon their thrust areas.

Common syllabus is not panacea

The idea of a common syllabus in higher education appears to be mooted in a few states for improving the quality of education in general across HEIs. The issue of inadequacy of the quality of education needs deeper evaluation. Though the syllabus lays the framework for carrying out the teaching-learning process, the quality is predominantly decided by the efficacy of teaching-learning processes for greater learning. The vision, competence and commitment of institutional leadership, teachers, and staff plays a critical role in improving the quality of education in HEIs. The rhetoric for having a common syllabus will eventually diminish the possibility of certain HEIs achieving distinctions.

Understandably, even by adopting the best of the syllabus for any programme in the world by an HEI, the state of education will not ameliorate unless those engaged in making learners learn do not carry out the teaching activities with full vigour, enthusiasm, and creativity. The role of institutional governance also affects the motivation and commitment of teachers and staff significantly. The insufficiency of academic merit and vision in an institutional leader can not enthuse the teaching human resource available with respective HEI. Thence, the qualitative improvement in education can take place largely through motivated, committed, creative and visionary leadership and teaching human resources of the HEI, however, the up-to-date syllabus is a prerequisite. The commonality of the syllabus shall make demean the role of teachers from particular HEI and reduce their academic participation. Having a uniform syllabus in different programmes offered by autonomous HEIs is not the panacea for improving the education quality.

Regulatory framework and HEIs together should get sensitized for enabling the institutions with merit centric leadership and competent teaching human resource along with encouraging and motivating ecosystem for ensuring learning in a happy and positive ambience. Cajoling the Universities and Deemed to be Universities for practising autonomy in true spirit could ignite the quest for excellence and inter-HEI competitiveness. The accelerated pace of accreditation of HEIs shall compel them for holistic improvement on all accounts.

****

CHAPTER VI

Gurus Being Outsourced in 'Vishwaguru' India

The recent proclamation about the outsourcing of teachers in higher education institutions is quite astounding, especially at a moment when the implementation of National Education Policy 2020 (NEP-2020) with a focus on motivated, energized and capable faculty is being pursued aggressively. All praises to NEP-2020 for acknowledging the criticality of faculty and calling for various initiatives to ensure that each faculty member is happy, enthusiastic, engaged, and motivated towards advancing her/his students, institution, and profession.

Unequivocally, the quality of education largely depends upon the commitment and involvement of teachers in the teaching-learning and allied processes in the education system. The conspicuous absence of Indian higher education institutions (HEIs) in top global rankings, despite a hopping number of brilliant minds in nearly 1.3 billion population, points to certain challenges faced by them. Among various challenges, the shortage of teachers in HEIs is the one limiting the quality of education.

Introspection of the shortage issue shows that it has become a permanent feature of higher education in the country. However, serious concerns have been demonstrated by the regulating authorities rapping HEIs from time to time. Unfortunately, not much could be achieved for whatsoever reason. The reasonable portion of teaching-learning processes carried out through contractual/ad-hoc/guest teachers has become a new norm. Hoping for the HEIs to thrive in such a situation is hallucinating.

NEP-2020 has rightly mandated for enhancing the Gross Enrolment Ratio (GER) for extending opportunities of higher education to a maximum number of aspirants. To increase access to higher education through a targeted GER of 50% by 2035, the additional 3.5 crores seats need to be added in HEIs. Undoubtedly, the demographic dividend available in India necessitates capacitating HEIs for meeting the aspirations of education seekers. But, the question remains, whether mere enrolment and award of certificates/degrees will educate the country to emerge as a world leader. The answer is a blunt NO!

Reasoning the prevalence of temporary teachers in HEIs leads to various factors for this precarious situation. However, the reasons could be different in public sector institutions and private sector institutions due to funding patterns. The HEIs in the private sector function in a self-financed mode, while the public sector HEIs get financed by public money available with Government. This causes the differing cost of education in such institutions. Interestingly, the regulatory bodies mandate similar norms for HEIs but their implementation is different in both types of institutions. Looking upon the salary norms, the regulatory framework does not discriminate between these types of institutions, but the basis of salary to teachers in the private sector varies hugely, while it is not so in the public sector HEIs. This facilitates private sector HEIs to hire teachers at mutually agreed compensation and the philosophy of teachers being temporary or permanent takes a backseat along with lesser concerns towards service conditions.

Public sector HEIs financed from public money are mandated for strict adherence of norms for hiring teachers as per prescribed pay scales & service conditions and employ teachers on a permanent basis or temporarily as contractual/ad-hoc/ guest/visiting faculty. The new arrangement of outsourcing of teachers in HEIs will engage a service provider too for being compensated financially for its services to provide teachers. The hiring of teachers as class III and class IV staff through outsourcing may ease out HEIs from the administrative hassles involved in recruiting temporary/regular teachers. However, it is disgraceful along with putting the additional financial burden – the service charges of the service provider – either on the HEIs or such teachers and shall always have the uncertainty of what is the actual compensation made to such teachers. Nonetheless, there will be new business opportunities for such service provider agencies that will supply teachers to HEIs.

The temporary teachers have meager compensation as compared to regular teachers in prescribed pay scales. Public sector HEIs, being unable to recruit teachers on regular scales for various reasons, resort to hiring teachers as contractual/ad-hoc/guest/visiting faculty with the intent of continued execution of teaching-learning processes. Obviously, the lesser compensation, uncertainty of remaining in service, and undefined service conditions are bound to keep these temporary teachers in a state of anxiety which hampers the quality of teaching-learning processes.

The mental state of teachers plays a crucial role in the quality of teaching-learning activities performed by them and such discontentment affects the overall quality of education for none of the fault of learner students. The job security and congenial environment for teaching and research are the key enablers for eliminating the occupational stresses of such temporary teachers, which requires to be taken care of at the earliest for sound mental health.

It goes without saying that those financially sound can afford an education at any price. Yet, the public sector HEIs remain a dream destination for those coming from a poor socio-economic background. Thence, any degeneration in the quality of education in public sector HEIs directly affects the opportunities of seeking excellent education for meritorious ones with poor financial backgrounds. The outstanding shortage of teachers in public sector HEIs is a ringing alarm. The quagmire can be gauged from a 2018 Parliament Report, according to which there were around 36% vacant posts out of total sanctioned posts numbering over 33 thousand in Central Universities, IITs, NITs, and IIITs functioning as centrally funded or in PPP mode. The statistics of vacant teacher posts may be much more perilous to the quality of education in state HEIs.

Irrespective of the causes of the non-availability of permanent teachers, expediting fair and transparent recruitment of regular teachers at the earliest is inevitable for the overall good of higher education in public sector HEIs. All attempts to increase the capacity of higher education without having teaching-learning enablers, especially the teachers, will belie the Prime Minister's humongous call for transforming India as Vishwa Guru.

****

CHAPTER VII

How feasible is Engineering Education without Physics and Mathematics?

All India Council for Technical Education (AICTE), the apex regulator for technical education in India has dismayed the engineering academics by making physics and mathematics non-obligatory subjects in the eligibility qualification for undergraduate engineering degree aspirants in its latest approval process for 2021.

The mandate is also given to the Universities to offer suitable bridge courses such as Mathematics, Physics, Engineering drawing, etc. for the students coming from diverse backgrounds to achieve desired learning outcomes of the undergraduate (UG) engineering degree programmes.

Nevertheless, in addition to aforesaid, the AICTE delineates the respective State Government/Affiliating University/Board to decide the eligibility criteria for entry-level Qualification for different Programmes/Courses.

Targeted beneficiaries

The prevailing eligibility qualifications for undergraduate engineering degree programme before the latest one of 2021 prescribed for physics and mathematics as the compulsory subjects in the secondary level examination along with a third subject from a specified list of subjects.

The unshackling of the rigid entry-level eligibility requirements by AICTE is stated to facilitate those possessing the aptitude as well as the background knowledge in certain branches of engineering and technology but were constrained to pursue the higher studies due to stringent compulsions of subjects in eligibility qualification.

The reliance is made on the flexibility envisaged by National Education Policy-2020 to the Universities to extend their support to such willing students to pursue a career in engineering and technology who were hitherto deprived owing to the barrier of subjects.

Despite the apparent intent to open up engineering education for all in secondary education, the education system has to assess the learning potential of the aspirants before terming them eligible for formal engineering education.

Every institutionalized education process has a set of subjects to be taught to the students which they have to pass after examinations.

The teaching methodology involved in the subjects of the engineering curriculum expects specific knowledge and competencies in the learners as prerequisites as the ultimate goal is to roll out competent engineering graduates.

Any lapses in prerequisite knowledge of learners might result in their difficulties to cope up with the engineering curriculum. It is not only disappointing to such beneficiaries but also incurs a loss of capacity utilization of demographic dividends available with the country.

In a democratic framework, the numbers matter a lot and in the case of a larger number of those struggling to complete engineering degrees due to gaps in certain prerequisite knowledge, the pressure will eventually fall on the educational institution to help them secure a degree.

There are umpteen instances, when the passing norms, repeated holding of examination, and other academic dilutions have emanated from the protests of failing students.

Specific eligibility for UG programmes

Indisputably, certain engineering degree programmes may be having specific eligibility requirements, but the much-sought cross-discipline higher education warrants basic knowledge of mathematical tools and analytical skills.

Certain references are made to the specific eligibility requirements of UG programmes in textile engineering, biotechnology, agriculture engineering, etc., where also, the apparent perusal of the syllabi shows that the knowledge of mathematics and physics is required.

Another reasoning for the dilution in prerequisites of eligibility qualification relies on the diploma holders seeking admission to UG engineering degree under lateral entry.

Factually, it is to be accepted that the diploma curriculum has adequate mathematics and physics courses enabling them to continue future learning. Thus, the knowledge base of diploma holders admitting to lateral entry cannot be compared with class XII students without physics and mathematics.

However, the differential eligibility requirements with prevailing prerequisites as per the respective UG engineering degree programme(s) will be a welcome move.

Thence, a candid assessment is required for ensuring that the change in eligibility prerequisites does not harm any innocent student who has never read the mathematics and physics landing into the engineering programme.

Moreover, the need is to remember that for pupils in general, formal education gets built on continuous procurement of knowledge sequentially with a series of prerequisites for carrying it forward and not merely on passion or aptitude alone.

Affect on learning outcomes

While diluting the rigidity in the entry-level qualification, the regulator has very carefully directed the engineering education providers to ensure that it should not affect the attainment of Learning Outcomes. Consequentially, the engineering institutions have to shift their focus from the quality of input unlike their practice of using an aggregate of Physics, Mathematics, Chemistry, or another entitled subject in class XII for assessing the quality of input i.e. the engineering aspirants.

Probing the stipulated curriculum of the UG engineering degree, the cumulative share of basic science courses and engineering science courses is found to be hovering around 30 per cent of the total programme credits.

Admittedly the engineering institutions build engineering graduates after teaching them a series of courses in program duration with a majority of them requiring the application of knowledge and analytical skills envisaged to be achieved in learning outcomes of physics and mathematics at the secondary level. Ergo, the conspicuous absence of prerequisite knowledge in the engineering aspirants is likely to make their pursuance of respective engineering degrees quite arduous.

The veracious reckoning of the dependence of output quality on input quality bespeaks the inseparable connection between the two, meaning thereby that the better is the quality of admitted students, so will be the quality of graduating students in general barring the exceptions. Thence, it sounds rhetorical to delink the output from input from the academic perspective.

Further, the insufficiency of knowledge sought from undergraduate degree programmes will have a cascading effect on the quality of the postgraduate and doctoral programmes.

Feasibility of bridge courses

In the absence of a well-thought framework through a model curriculum, the apex regulator's decree to the educational institutions for taking care of its move of unbinding the eligibility qualifications for UG engineering degree through bridge courses looks formalistic.

The Indian model of engineering education has stipulated a period of engineering degree programmes duly populated with the courses necessary to achieve the respective programme outcomes. The consideration of prerequisites happens to be the foundation block in laying down the complete curriculum for such programmes.

There are feasibilities of offering bridge courses by offering them before existing courses requiring physics and mathematics knowledge or by replacing some of the existing courses with such courses. In the former case, the students will be burdened additionally and make it difficult to pursue the rest of the courses with the same efficacy as compared to those who do not require such bridge courses. While in the latter case the dislodging students from some courses may weaken their professional competencies.

Evaluating flexibility

Offering increased flexibility in terms of freedom to students who choose subjects other than Mathematics, Physics and are from different domains might have practical difficulties in executing this model at entry-level to the UG engineering degree programme.

Howbeit, the flexibility in the later stage of the UG engineering degree is always feasible by offering interdisciplinary subjects with sound foundational engineering knowledge and it shall help achieve the objective of National Education Policy-2020.

On account of the desired Graduate Attributes and Programme Outcomes of the UG engineering degrees, the proclaimed flexibility for admitting the students devoid of physics and mathematics knowledge seems paradoxical.

Employability

Looking at the employability of engineering graduates being not more than 80 per cent as per certain reports, the concerns for improving the overall quality are inevitable. The efforts for improving the quality of engineering education have been constantly pushing for various measures through a proper mix of theory and practical subjects from science, humanities, professional core, and interdisciplinary areas along with hands-on training, internships, etc.

These are based on the premise of core competencies of admitting students that have been meticulously ingrained by the secondary education system. Unequivocally, the opening of engineering education to the students who have not undertaken even the subjects of physics and mathematics will limit them from understanding the prevailing curriculum effectively unless complete remodelling is not done.

The focus of the National Education policy-2020 for opening up education and making it multidisciplinary necessitates a series of changes without sacrificing the quality of the existing education model. However, the integration of the experiences had from the successes and lapses of the existing engineering education is critically indispensable to make it much more productive and useful for society at large.

Undoubtedly, the changes are required for increasing access to engineering education to all those possessing passion for it, but sacrificing the fundamental requirements of such education demands a holistic view. Also, the exodus of students away from engineering education and the degeneration in its quality due to its sudden opening up in the country along with other reasons should be considered by the apex regulator for exploiting the full potential of youth for good of the nation.

****

CHAPTER VIII

How institutions can evolve to overcome learning gaps in online education in time of COVID-19?

There is an urgent need for educational institutions in India to evolve and develop suitable strategies and alternative arrangements to compensate for the loss faced by the students and parents following the drawbacks in online education amid the prevailing Covid circumstances and the great divide in society. On account of the prevailing circumstances, the truth about the spread of Coronavirus infection is becoming a matter of great debate in the world's second-largest populous nation—India.

The trust deficit seems to emanate from the government's mandate for preventing COVID on one hand and the holding of election rallies by the responsible functionaries of the government at the Centre and states in the assembly elections underway in five states as well as those held in the year 2020, on the other. Different states are professing for night curfew, reducing attendance at workplaces, closure of educational institutions, stringent enforcement of COVID prevention norms, etc to handle the reported upsurge in COVID infection. Simultaneously, the aggressive campaign for vaccinating the citizens is also in progress.

Unequivocally, the commitment of the government at the Centre and states to prevent the spread of COVID by enforcement of certain measures and expedient delivery of vaccines as per norms cannot be questioned.

Changed Perception of Online Education

The recent protests by the students, teachers, and management of educational institutions together against the proclaimed closure of institutions while compelling them to go for the online mode of education reveal contrasting public perceptions.

Looking back, it is evident that the educational institutions were closed since the first lockdown in March 2020, and the education system struggled for its continued delivery through online mode followed by the online or proforma assessment to promote students to the next higher class.

With time, the stakeholders understood the limitations of the much-hyped online mode of education delivery in India reeling under a significant digital divide owing to the varying socio-economic conditions, lack of requisite IT infrastructure, absence of peer interactions, and facilities at the institution & student ends. By now, there are well-settled arguments against the efficacy of online education deliveries due to the poor quality of learning from it along with questionable integrity of the learning assessment mechanisms.

Undoubtedly, the teachers and students both are convinced that it is extremely difficult to acquire the requisite knowledge and learning levels through online teaching. As a result, with the COVID settling down, all stakeholders desperately wanted the educational institutions to open and the resumption of offline classes was welcomed.

Endangered Viability of Self-Financed Education System

The COVID-driven closure in the past has seen that the teachers and staff in the self-financed education institutions faced a crisis of non-payment of salaries to them. The inadequate receipt of the fees from students led to the insufficiency of funds with the management to pay the salaries at par with pre-COVID times. In the absence of any source of funding except student fees in the self-financed institution, this fear of non-payment of salaries to teachers and staff of the institution is not unfounded.

Thence the closure of the institution will not affect the financial receipts of the management, teachers, and staff till the student fees keep pouring in at the normal rate. But the possibility of reduction of receipts on account of relaxation to students for reduced/delayed fee payment to the institution because of the poor economic conditions of parents/guardians from COVID centric closures cannot be ruled out and thus questioning the viability of survival of self-financed institutions.

Cues from Online Classes and Offline Examinations

As the lockdown got relaxed gradually in the last year, the regulators started devising a suitable mechanism for assessing the learning levels of the students in respective courses. The offline examinations were held with necessary arrangements in educational institutions. Nevertheless, in the number of programs and classes, the students were promoted without examination.

In view of lesser learning from online classes, the education system constantly observed the demand of the students for not holding offline examinations for online teaching. Finally, the system prevailed and the conduction of offline examination after the online classes, made the students think that their final assessment warrants adequate learning with them.

Also, the conduction of competitive examinations for the students aspiring for higher education as well as for jobs in offline mode sensitized them about the fact that eventually, the requisite knowledge and learning levels are essentially required to succeed.

Absence of Arrangements to Compensate Learning Losses

Seemingly, the prominent worry of the students is about the learning loss incurred in the online mode of teaching. The inadequacy of learning in online teaching is evinced through various media reports. This learning gap is immensely important and needs to be taken care of by the education providers before marching the students to the next levels.

Nonetheless, the conspicuous absence of any institutional arrangements for overcoming the learning deficiencies nucleates a feeling that those who are offered online education will ultimately be losers vis-a-vis those who will take the same in offline mode later after the pandemic is over.

With the competitions becoming stiffer day by day, the students are becoming increasingly conscious about their knowledge from respective course/programme. Thus, it is pertinent for educational institutions to evolve suitable strategies to overcome the learning gaps created on account of the compelling circumstances in which online education is continued.

The point of view of students, teachers, and those running the education institutions about the losses incurring in terms of knowledge, salaries, and other financial receipts for ensuring institutional viability respectively is essential.

Also, the changing perspective of the stakeholders about takeaways from online education necessitates serious thinking at the level of regulating bodies and educational institutions for delineating well-laid holistic regulations to ensure that the students get ample opportunities to equip themselves with prescribed knowledge to remain at par with those who are taught in the post-pandemic era.

It seems inevitable to practice living with the disease in an appropriately crafted education framework and not disrupt the education as and when.

****

CHAPTER IX

Disruptions call for remodeling examinations and evaluation strategies amid COVID-19

The country is again disquieted with the COVID upsurge engulfing it. As a part of the efforts to break the chain of virus spread, the part or complete closure of various sectors, including the education sector, is enforced across the country. Taking a trip down memory lane, the similar closure of education institutions disrupted the teaching-learning and examination processes of session 2019-20 since March 25, 2020. This is the second academic session 2020-21 in a series that is facing the brunt of COVID.

With examination time coming closer, the debates buzzed around for quite some time to not hold the already scheduled board examinations at class 10 and 12 levels. Consequently, some of the education boards announced the cancellation/rescheduling of the board examinations considering the panic in students, parents, teachers, and school staff alike to end the stress of incertitude. In many cases, the board examinations of class 12 have been postponed while these have been scrapped off for class 10.

Digital interventions

Introspecting the scenario of the year-long unsettled state of education institutions due to lockdown enforced last year in the country, the loss of learning of students due to shattered teaching-learning activities is concerning.

Unequivocally, the online teaching-learning activities came to rescue their sacrifice, but they lacked access and equity due to the prevailing digital divide and varying socio-economic conditions of Indian society. The inherent limitations of digital mode of interactions such as the inadequate IT facilities with all students and teachers, absence of peer-to-peer interaction, ghost-like teaching, lack of physical mentoring, detestable screen-time requirement, etc. led to reduced knowledge gain by the students.

Also, the sacrosanct examination and evaluation resorting to online mode for quantifying learning levels of students in the traditional education system got unconsecrated. Despite numerous IT solutions coming up for carrying out proctored examinations, the dependence on hugely varying IT facilities at student and institution end has limited the attainment of complete fairness in the evaluation of student learning levels.

Undoubtedly a lot of educational innovations have been made through digital interventions, but the insufficiency of such remote learning and other associated facilitators made learners crazy for on-campus teaching-learning-examination-evaluation activities.

The students and teachers both desperately want to have on-campus teaching-learning activities, but the schools and colleges could not hold the on-campus classes due to the COVID restrictions imposed in respective states. Some schools and colleges became functional from their campuses for a short duration before the second surge COVID compelled for their closure again about one year later the first lockdown.

Nevertheless, in such frequent disruptions, the online education gave respite to the learners as well as teachers, but when it comes to examination for assessing the learning, the offline is still harped upon by regulators though contested by students.

Remodel assessment process

The ongoing conflict between the education system and students as its beneficiaries in respect to the rationale of holding offline examinations for online teaching necessitates holistic thinking. For a cogent solution to the problems arising out of sudden disruptions like those faced since last year, there is a need to understand some of the core issues and look for solutions.

The purpose of examination in formal education should be discerned as an approach to assess the learning levels of the learners after the prescribed content is taught. Usually, there will be 2 to 3 hours of examination for particular subjects with the complete syllabus covered in the respective question papers which are supposed to be answered in the duly invigilated environment. Howbeit, during the session, the mid-session/term examinations are conducted with part syllabus coverage as part of continuous evaluation but are not given due consideration in the final board examinations of secondary and senior secondary level. Accordingly, the performance of examinees in the question paper indicates the extent of learning and knowledge level possessed by them. Cumulative performance indices decide division/grade/pass/fail for them, in particular, class end-of-session examinations, which are used in the future for moving on to the next class, getting employment, etc.

In order to find the solution to replacing the final examinations as tools for learning level assessments in any class up to the senior secondary level of education, let us try to reason out the following;

- Why the continuous evaluation does not replace the final examination?
- How does the final examination of 2-3 hours entitle for better assessment vis-a-vis mid-session/term examinations for particular syllabus coverage?
- Why can't the number of mid-session/term examinations be not made rigorous and sacrosanct like board examinations and synthesized as a replacement of final examination?
- Why can't the pattern of questions in online examinations be made of such a kind that it is akin to open book examination such that no proctoring is required?

In the precarious state of online education, academics must contemplate three key aspects. Firstly, let us depend solely upon the continuous evaluation by holding portion-by-portion examinations in a sacrosanct manner. Secondly, the preparation of questions is carried out diligently to extract the real worthiness of learners and make it an even open book examination and get rid of any proctoring in the online examination. Thirdly, the limitations imposed by the digital divide can be partly taken care of by creating nationwide mutual cooperation among education providers for sharing their digital infrastructure. This shared digital infrastructure could facilitate access to regional students calling for it is irrespective of whether they are from a respective school or not.

The repeated disruptions in classroom teaching-learning processes on account of pandemics essentially call for brooding amongst academics and regulators for evolving an affirmative action plan in which online education is integrated with online examination throughout the session. It is high time to realise and act upon to circumvent the disturbances in academic sessions incurring any loss of opportunity to the student community in new normal. To bring an end to the anxiety among students, the online education model should inevitably have student assessment through well-articulated online examination system regulations without any variability. Seemingly the on-line education is to stay back and obligates effective framework for all levels of education so that students are not panicked frequently time and again.

****

CHAPTER X

Losing sheen of Guru Devo Bhava: An Introspection

Above age-old Sanskrit, shloka is universally accepted across India to mark the deep respect and gratitude to the teachers as Gurus. This also reiterates the role of teachers in the life of all and embellishes a whole lot of teachers in the formal education system too.

The recent incident of a teacher scolding a certain set of students in the premier technological institution in independent India does not augur well. The indecent remarks made by any teacher to students are uncalled for. It is appalling to witness such incidents as these were for the academically weak students. Further, it points to the polluted mental set up especially when these students belonged to the SC, ST, and PWD communities as per media reports.

Reasoning indignity in academics

Unfortunately, the higher education of the country is not witnessing such demeanor of custodians of educating younger generation i.e. the teachers for the first time, instead, there are umpteen numbers of instances when teachers have crossed the threshold of decency and mistreated their disciples. Quite often students have been complaining about the teachers carrying positive and negative biases towards selective students during teaching, examination, evaluation, and mentoring. Unequivocally, the bias does not have any place in the sacrosanct teaching-learning-examination-evaluation processes. The teachers are supposed to conduct ethically and demonstrate their fairness with integrity to nurture the similar traits of being fair, ethical, moral, and help in ingraining the best values in their students.

The unequal handling of students by teachers could be ascribed to their

- weak academic credentials,
- poor performance in examinations,
- poor response in classroom interactions,
- poor financial standing leading to fewer learning resources,
- deficient IT equipment and other facilities,
- caste-based discriminations,
- social perception, etc.

Interestingly the most of the factors responsible for their subjugation to partisanship are inherently congenital. Innocent human birth in any family is put through particular social order for which the newborn is not at fault, instead, it is the society's creation despite knowing the fact that every life is equal in all aspects. In fact, for any child, the economic condition of the family dictates the quality of life, the standard of living, access to education and other opportunities, facilities, social circle, etc. that is also not in control at the time of birth. Therefore, the teachers being in the most responsible role for creating future human beings to sustain the civilization and take the society forward should ponder upon the sensitive issues humanely.

Does reservation polarize education institutions?

It has been the insufficient presence of people from certain communities of the society in different sectors and various levels that pushed for creating special provisions in the Indian constitution. The constitution has Article 46 to enable the state to promote and take special care of the educational and economic interests of weaker sections of the society and protect them from social injustice and exploitation via reservations in India.

Nevertheless, the Government has enforced reservation for so many decades in admissions in educational institutions and employment but the inadequate representation of these communities till now entails thorough rumination. The under-representation of people from SC/ST/OBC and other weaker sections of society is explicitly prevalent in educational institutions which could be attributed to various factors including discriminatory treatment. Therefore, the statutory provisions created through constitutional processes should not be envied.

Undoubtedly there is stiff competition for seeking admission in higher education in the country and students from all sections strive hard to get it based on their merit in competitive examinations. The statutory reservation eases the admission to the students from reserved categories even with lesser merit and others take umbrage for not getting opportunity despite their superior merit. This creates a veiled antipathy among students, however, there are ample reasons for grant of reservation and should not be brought into discussion for maintaining harmony in the education system. Sometimes the thinking and actions of the teachers & officials of education institutions are found discriminatory on the basis of social origin and ridges are noticeable. The gravitas of discrimination is evinced from the fact that in February 2021, the University Grants Commission directed higher education institutions to devise a mechanism to redress caste-based grievances. The presence of statutory authorities like different National /

State commissions for SC/ST, OBC, women, children, and other deprived sections corroborates the necessity felt by the Government for special care required for such sections.

Implications of ill-treatment

In general, higher education usually enrolls students of more than 18 years of age i.e. at which they are entitled to exercise the franchise and participate in the functioning of democracy. Thence, any grudges nucleated in the student minds during the course of pious teaching-learning process for being born in families classified as SC/ST/ Backwards or having physical disabilities due to reasons beyond their control are likely to culminate into hatred against some and try to pull apart the social fabric of the society. The privilege given in the form of reservation and others makes such students hypersensitive to any differential treatment by either a few teachers, peers, institutional governance, etc.

The perceptions developed by such students based on day-to-day interactions make them realize their social background and other limitations beyond their control. As a result, sufferings like depression due to failures, lacking in exhibiting performances comparable to others, peaceful & violent fight for justice, etc. are observed and may even culminate in students bringing an end to their life as was in Rohit Vemula's case.

In a large number of cases, the discrimination met to students by the teachers at any stage instills ill feelings and a sense of insecurity. The negative perception of such students changes their attitude towards others in real life. As often as not, this is discernible in the form of their biases and taking special measures to protect those similar to them.

The contemplation of the precarious situation arising out of discrimination reveals the creation of a vicious loop that starts from the students getting distanced from teachers psychologically. Consecutively, the widening of the gap between student and teachers inculcates a lack of confidence to get their doubts resolved, followed by their poor performance in assessment tools, which results in creating a pool of academically weak students who may be subjected to remedial classes, such identification is stigmatic to them, causing aversion of students from studies that makes them perform badly and the gap between student and teacher further widens.

Soul searching by Teachers

Chanakya said "A teacher is never ordinary. Holocaust and creation flourish in his lap" (Translated from Hindi quote- *Shikhak kabhi sadharan nahi hota. Pralay aur nirman uski god mein palte hain.*)

This popular quote is to sensitize teachers about their roles and responsibilities towards civilization, however, they are well aware of their pre-eminence. But the sporadic occurrences of misdemeanor by few teachers result in a loss of respect and dignity of the whole community of mentors. The shame brought by the misconduct of select teachers warrants self-appraisal by all academics and their regulators. Any misuse of the freedom and authority vested in the mentoring community has long-lasting bad imprints on younger minds.

Teachers ought to understand that the students consider them as role models for which they have to exercise restraints and self-imposed restrictions to prove worthy of student expectations. Society's grace of putting teachers at par with God decrees for high moral values, exuberant, inspirational, ethical conduct, absence of biases, high integrity, transparency, and commitment in them for rolling out a better society.

Teachers should contemplate bringing complete equity, free-thinking, and freedom of expression on campuses and sincerely endeavour for getting rid of the setting up of bodies/committees within institutions for safeguarding the interests of certain sections of society. Ideally, the educational institution campus should offer equal treatment to all without fail. The moot point is that the teachers have to bring change within them and ensure ethical practices for well being of students as setting up bodies/committees to safeguard the interests of certain sections has proved to be ornamental and ineffective in many cases.

Indisputably the relationship between teacher and taught are pious and all efforts are required from teachers & officials of educational institutions to sew up their relations with fairness, transparency, integrity, selfless support, handholding, and care. Teachers have to muster the strength to thwart any attempt of disturbing the serenity of campuses and their virtuous relations with students as the educational institutions can only shine by the pride, hard work, achievements, and pristine glory of their teachers and students.

For creating a healthy and vibrant society, the teaching fraternity should resolve to demonstrate decency, tolerance, discipline, and merit-centric actions with high integrity without any kind of discrimination towards their students.

****

CHAPTER XI

Education in Times of COVID: Shun End of Course Final Examinations

Despite the hesitancy of the education providers, the frequent closure of educational institutions neccesitates online mode of examination for assessing the retention and application of knowledge of students. The educational institutions were coerced to opt for online offerings and develop/adopt certain online platforms and protocols for continuing their teaching-learning-evaluation activities. The potential threat of the spread of pandemic made the conventional pen-paper examination for end of course summative assessment infeasible and walkthrough was allowed to next higher classes based on some formative assessment. Nevertheless, the formative assessment is not carried out with the same rigour in all institutions primarily due to the absence of an appropriate and foolproof framework for it and secondly due to other factors such as the insufficiency of teachers, quality of teachers, sense of responsibility in teachers, institutional governance, student freedom, etc. As a result, the education regulators and the institutions endeavored hard to hold the final examinations in offline mode as per the prescribed academic calendars, but the fear psychosis in stakeholders necessitated the frequent deferments that devastated the academic calendar and rendered anxiety in students.

The uncertainties in the examination system affecting students socially and psychologically have restricted their holistic development and learning capabilities. In the present circumstances, the students rarely study exclusively and there is the least conflict between their education and work/family/personal obligations as compared to the on-campus learning activities. In total, the prolonged absence of teaching-learning activities in campuses of educational institutions is limiting their performance and output quality. The education system as a whole being in firefighting mode for two academic sessions now needs to devise an infallible mechanism for validating the student knowledge and abilities of its application in such a disrupted environment. The accreditation bodies should also ponder upon the challenges faced in holding summative assessments of learning outcomes in students through conventional print-based examinations.

For strategizing the solutions to the prevailing problems, which may also crop up in the future, it is sine qua nan to start from the very purpose of examinations for learning authentication. Unequivocally, the purpose of education is to impart knowledge and capability of use of the knowledge in real life. The teaching-learning process is usually gradual and peace by peace transfer of knowledge gets ingrained in the students. The direct and indirect assessment tools essentially compel the students to continue the study and help the education system to authenticate the extent of learning. The prevalence of formative assessment during the academic session to assess the progressive learning of students and summative assessment at the end of the session is quite old and accepted well by all the stakeholders. Till the end of the course final examinations were held smoothly, the look for an alternative to conventional pen-paper final examinations was not imperative. Nonetheless, the difficulties faced in holding final examinations in pen-paper format warrant requisite changes in assessment and evaluation strategies.

While looking for alternatives, it entails a question of why the evaluation of knowledge, its retention, and ability to apply by students can not solely rely upon the formative assessment which is carried out at different intervals across the session till the course is complete. Let us compare the two modes of assessment namely formative and summative to reach the substitution of the conventional final examinations.

Considering the final course end examination of three hours and comparing it with the three formative assessment examinations of one hour each it is evident that the total period of examination for assessing the student learning in the respective course is the same. Thence, the summative assessment of three hours can be prima-facie replaced by more than three formative assessments during the course teaching.

Further, for any course, the coverage in frequent formative assessments is limited to smaller portions of the complete syllabus which is comparable to the course coverage of the summative assessment conducted at the course completion.

Undoubtedly, the integrity of formative assessments in the majority of cases is not comparable to the end-of-course summative assessment and is concerning. This can be easily corrected by the setting up of a stringent framework for formative assessment of student learning by use of available internet-powered digital technologies.

Under such circumstances, the efforts ought to be made for strengthening the formative assessment tools of direct and indirect type both. The discontinuance of physical classroom activities and adaptation of online examinations in place of pen and paper type invigilated examinations offers a congenial environment for redefining the formative assessment tools. Moreover, the current use of digital technologies for online examinations for authenticating student learning paves the way for creating digital platforms for frequent learning assessments of students during the teaching of course.

The efforts to shun the final end examinations of pen-paper type involve consideration of the following issues;

- specifying the formative assessment tools in line with prescribed learning outcomes
- student perception on the continuous assessment being a true indicator of their learning
- teacher perception on the continuous assessment replacing term-end examination
- digital divide to ensure access to all in case of remote conduction of periodical learning assessment
- limitations at the student and institution end in practicing formative assessment tools
- technological challenges in the creation of suitable robust internet-based access controlled & proctored digital framework for fair and transparent assessment
- authenticity of online examinations and other practices for learning level assessment
- fairness of online evaluation processes
- restricting the possible malpractices
- accreditation requirements

Thus, it will be prudent on the part of the academic community and education regulators to encourage greater uptake of online examinations in the formal education system. The cue can be had from the computer-based competitive examinations like JEE, NEET, CLAT, etc. being held successfully for admissions in different courses. It is an opportune time to create enabling robust framework for using digitally enabled formative assessment tools to evaluate the learning levels of students progressively in the respective course and get rid of the pen-paper type conventional final end-of-course examinations. This frequent learning assessment of students during the course teaching is likely to improve the extent of student engagement in teaching-learning processes and improve the learning levels of students as well as teacher involvement, provided it is conducted with the highest integrity, fairness, and transparency.

****

CHAPTER XII

Calibrate education in Corona aftermath

The 21st century started with the outbreak of severe acute respiratory syndrome (SARS) in 2003 ensued by H1N1 swine flu in 2009, Middle East Respiratory Syndrome (MERS) in 2012, Ebola virus in 2014, and finally the most dreaded one being COVID-19 continuing since the end of 2019. Fortunately, India did not feel the heat of either of these outbreaks except the latest one i.e. COVID-19. The enforcement of lockdown from 24th March 2020 impacted all sectors adversely. The closure of educational institutions disrupted teaching-learning activities and jolted a whole lot of students from the lowest to the highest level of formal education in academic session 2019-20, however, the disruption was adequately handled through the assessment based on previous performance and deferred conduction of final Board & University examinations for terminal classes like final examinations for class XII, graduation, post-graduation, etc.

In the meantime, the online mode of teaching was adapted for continuing the teaching-learning processes and acted as a panacea for education providers in sustaining the academic session 2020-21. But for many, it remained an illusion due to the unavailability of adequate internet and facilities like computers, laptops, smartphones, etc. The digital divide and varying socio-economic conditions came as the deterrent to the success of online teaching-learning activities. Nevertheless, the country had no other option than to continue with online activities despite knowing its limitations. Undoubtedly, the regulatory bodies tried their level best to ease out the learning processes to the extent of truncating the syllabus. The virtual conduction of the laboratory was also conceived and this continued to meet out the laboratory requirements. The small number of COVID infection cases and fatalities in the year 2020 raised the confidence level of the country's governance that resulted in the opening of the educational institutions to resume teaching activities on campus, though with certain care.

Suddenly, the massive surge of the pandemic in March 2021 called for the closure of educational institutions again, and the teaching-learning activities got discontinued in the latter half of the academic session 2020-21. The enforcement of no examination policy up to class XI and deferment of class XII board examinations and other higher classes became inevitable by many boards that could not complete these prior to the second surge of March 2021.

Unequivocally, the uncertainty creeping in the minds of those who are in class XII and aspiring to seek admission in graduate degree programmes of engineering, medical, law, etc. is atrocious. There are a good number of students that choose to take a drop in the year 2020 due to precariousness of COVID-19 havoc resulting in extraordinary delays in commencement of academic session 2020-21 and decided to try admission in academic session 2021-22 hoping that the situation will be normal by then. Nonetheless, this is proving fallacious! It seems that the virus is here to stay longer.

Indisputably, it is the second consecutive academic session when the students have not learnt their subjects of respective classes well. The continued firefighting with

COVID-19 has not allowed for much preparedness on the part of the educational institutions as well as the students in the second academic session of 2020-21 too. Indeed, the efficacy of online teaching stands questionable. The courses involving laboratory learning have felt the brunt of online teaching heavily, as the student hands-on sessions in laboratories can not be substituted by virtual laboratories. Altogether, the learning deficiencies are ought to be there in the students due to the focus being majorly on:

- self-learning;
- the institutional facilitation being limited to online interactions;
- limited IT facilities and internet;
- changing family conditions;
- absence of moral support from colleagues, etc.

The implications of the insufficient knowledge will be felt in the form of deficient competencies of such students of 2019-20 and 2020-21 academic sessions whose sufferings are attributed to COVID, in proving their worth for a particular qualification possessed by them. Patently, this COVID menace will be over after some time and living humans will pretermit the hypochondriasis and the horrifying loss of life around in the months of April – May 2021 due to it. Once normalcy restores, these affected students of two academic sessions marred by pandemic will have to essentially compete with others of past and future who have undertaken similar education without any panic. The learning level differences amidst those having passed similar classes/examinations may create troubles in the longer run. Therefore a suitable mechanism is required to compensate the learning losses by students themselves or by the educational institution.

From the education perspective, it is also the disturbing timelines of academic sessions, that is concerning along with many facets of the COVID aftermath. Thus, the key issues needing attention are;

- To make up the learning gaps in students due to non-conduction of proper classes;
- To compensate for the loss of learning of those reeling under the digital divide;
- To make the continuous online learning assessments sacrosanct and acceptable substitute for pen-paper based final examinations;
- To reschedule the shifted timelines;
- To restore the confidence and esteem of learners who have felt the adversities of COVID;
- To facilitate education for those facing financial hardships in sustaining education;
- To educate the young generation for meeting out the catastrophic pandemics with minimum loss of life;
- To amend the curriculum to ensure that learners are sensitive enough towards sustainable developments;
- To equip the institutions and students for online teaching-learning processes;
- To rejuvenate the self-financed educational institutions becoming unviable due to lack of admissions, students dropping out because of poor financial conditions, and reduction in fee receipts.

Desirably, the educational institutions must set up well-thought-out action plans to ensure that the enrolled as well as passed out students of COVID-affected academic sessions get opportunities to learn the missing portions and possess the prescribed course outcomes. Institutional measures are essentially required to conquer over the extermination caused by COVID due to the unavailability of oxygen and healthcare facilities, failing which it will prove to be absolutely unpropitious to the growth of humanity and civilization. The regulators of education for all levels should inevitably ponder upon the concerned stakeholders and palliate the damage incurred to the younger generation of the country which is blessed with a 37-year advantage of demographic dividend. The opportunity loss on account of youth remaining disengaged from their pursuits of getting educated well warrants strategizing for immediate correction. The loss of youth potential on day to day basis may push the country out of its mission of achieving the targeted $5 trillion economy.

Let's deliberate and discuss extensively to create a well-laid framework based on the holistic considerations for negotiating the past, present, and future disruptions in the education system lest it is late again.

****

CHAPTER XIII

Scrapping of class 12 exams calls for onerous responsibility of redrafting evaluation strategy

The scrapping of CBSE class 12 board examinations on the first day of June in 2021 has made it a historical day in the school education of India. Unequivocally, the decision brought an end to the disquietude caused by the buzz on account of exam or no exam debate in the terminal class of formal school education. The catastrophic second wave of COVID-19 incurring a huge loss of life primarily due to the unpreparedness of the healthcare system unsettled the whole country and impacted the education sector severely.

Given the school education being catered separately by states, the disruptions in the education system were tholed differently by each state through the online classes, online examinations, and pen-paper examinations during the opening for a short stint since March 24, 2020. The decisions taken for promoting the students to upper classes without examinations became a new normal. However, it was not enforced uniformly in all examinations.

Accolades to the regulatory bodies for sustaining the massive pressure of no-examinations in the last academic session 2019-20 and continuing with the long pervading practice of the proper pen-paper examinations at least for the terminal classes i.e. the classes for which certificate, diploma, degree, etc. is issued with statutory validity and acceptance across the world. In hindsight, the end-of-course summative assessment was inevitable in the absence of a credible and foolproof formative assessment system for evaluating student learning.

Surprisingly, even with the delayed commencement of the current academic session 2020-21 in online mode, the model of evaluating learning level in respective classes was not amended and the need for end-of-course, final examination continued like those in pre-pandemic times. Consequently, the examination boards announced their end-of-course final examinations starting from the beginning of the year 2021. The smart examination board like that of Bihar completed their class 10 & 12 board examinations in the first quarter of 2021 and declared results for class 12 and class 10 on March 26, 2021, and April 05, 2021, respectively while the majority of state examination boards, CBSE, and ICSE could not hold board examinations for these classes.

The decision to cancel class 10 examinations by CBSE in the mid of April 2021 when the pandemic was at its peak, triggered the debate for examination or no examination in class 12 too. The majority of states reeling under lockdowns or corona curfews compelled the respective examination boards to cancel class 10 examinations and reschedule their class 12 examinations, however, the CBSE continued with discussions with stakeholders on the model & feasibility of examination before arriving at a final decision. The Chhattisgarh board announced a novel model of open book examination for its class 12 students commencing from June 1, 2021, nevertheless, this started debate about the fairness of the assessment.

Looking back at the chronology of the events, it is apparent that except Delhi state which called for vaccination of class 12 students before examination or its cancellation, the majority of state boards and CBSE continued with their will to hold class 12 examinations, maybe in a different format and at the time when COVID gets controlled. The stakeholders were divided on the models prepared by CBSE for holding examinations and the arguments of not adapting the alternative mode of examination as it would not do justice were also heard. But, the intent of cancellation of class 12 examinations was not evident till the apex meeting was held for taking a final call on the issue on June 1, 2021.

Now, with the cancellation of class 12 examinations of CBSE, the state examination boards are under the obligation of revisiting their proclamations of holding class 12 examinations. The decision of cancellation of class 12 examinations is said to have come with a caveat that CBSE will be evolving methodology for declaring class 12 results on the basis of some objective criteria with the provision for the interested ones to appear in these examinations at later dates, howbeit the final framework for it is awaited from the CBSE.

Undoubtedly, there are reasons to welcome the cancellation due to fear created by COVID, but brooding on the implications of cancellations is not uncalled for. With the unprecedented call of cancellation of the apex board examination of class 12 in the Indian schooling system, the concerned students and their parents will have a series of questions that may make them anxious again. The academic community could also have divided opinions on the issue. But the fact remains that the sanctity of learning assessment and award of pass certificates with certain marks/grades by the examination boards based on methodology getting evolved now after the classes are over is questionable.

First, the fairness and integrity of internal examinations held in schools across the country in classes 11 and 12 are not infallible. The biases of school teachers towards students on account of different considerations cannot be purged out of student minds. Also, in the majority of cases, the shifted focus of class 11-12 students towards competitive examinations like JEE, NEET, CLAT, etc. pushes them to ignore school internal examinations, which are likely to leave a permanent imprint on their class 12 certificate now in the changed circumstances.

Second, the fairness of school examination assessment in case of the students who merely get registered in school in class 11-12 for appearing in final board examination i.e. dummy schools may be difficult to ascertain.

Third, the difficulty may also be felt in compiling the internal assessments in case of the students changing schools in between classes 11 and 12.

Fourth, the variance in school assessments like liberal, moderate, and strict award of marks is likely to land up in a situation where marks are not a true indicator of learning levels and the credibility of marks in pass certificates gets lost. Preparing inter-se-merit based on the school evaluation system will be an arduous task for the higher education institutions in granting admissions.

Fifth, the grant of autonomy to schools to assess their students without accrediting their capabilities for doing so may not augur well with all students, and the students toiling hard to prove their academic capabilities may not get justice.

Apart from the above, these pass certificates of the present class 12 students that will be issued without common public examination of the respective boards, will not be comparable to those issued after proper public examinations in the past and future.

At present, with the Centre scrapping the CBSE examination of class 12, the state boards need to ponder upon its implications in the context of the lockdown and pandemic in their territory, integrity of schools, education, and evaluation pattern followed by schools in the past two years, and demography. The out of the ordinary decision of canceling CBSE examinations burdens it with the onerous responsibility of redrafting the evaluation strategy that is fair, transparent, and realistic so that none of the students feel the pinch of pandemic across his/her life.

****

CHAPTER XIV

Exam Hesitancy: Drawbacks in e-learning seem to have shaken confidence of students for undertaking exams

Undoubtedly, the devastating second wave of the COVID-19 pandemic in India has inundated all with anxiety to the extent that the realization of normal activities appears a dream. The fear psychosis inculcated from the past and forecast of the third wave is dominating all spheres of life, including the education system. It is more than a year since the education system started experimenting with the teaching, learning, examination, and evaluation processes at primary, secondary, and tertiary education levels. Among various decisions of scrapping the final examinations taken to date, the cardinal one happens to be the scrapping of class 12 examinations, especially in a country where the board examinations of class 10 and 12 have been sacrosanct since time immemorial.

The students calling for no examinations time and again with support for such calls from different quarters points to the permeating examination hesitancy in them. Because the practice of no examination has been infrequent in the Indian education system as the evidence of examinations being essentially held despite academic sessions getting delayed are in abundance. The tendency of skipping examination betokens a precarious situation of students evading their learning assessments and marching ahead without formal examination.

Saying no to examinations in the present setup with partial or full dependence on the end-of-course examinations inexorably warrants introspection especially in classes for which certificates are issued by examining boards or universities.

Practice of student learning assessment

It is worth mentioning that the prevailing practice of centralized examination for student learning assessments emanates from the intent to have uniformity and fairness in the assessment processes while eliminating chances of institution-centric subjectivity. Philosophically, there is no issue with the education institutions evaluating the learning levels of their students for the award of final mark sheets/certificates as the teaching-learning processes are carried out by these institutions. But this may require requisite statutory provisions, preparedness of the institutions, and recognition so that every school/ institution acts as a board/university and awards its mark sheets and certificates with global validity.

Thus the practice of promoting students without examinations in the last two academic sessions transfers the sole responsibility of student learning on the institutions i.e. the rigour with which the teaching-learning processes have been carried out.

Reasoning examination hesitancy

The lapses in the online teaching activities due to limited resources and the digital divide between the students and teachers alike are quite known in the country. Despite recurrent proclamations of smooth conduction of online teaching-learning activities, the academics know the ground reality that the actual teaching-learning activities have not been up to the mark since the first closure of education institutions in March 2020. This seems to have shaken the confidence of students for undertaking end-of-course examinations and the instances of students calling for their progression to higher class without examination are conspicuous.

In fact, it owes to the panic caused by the first wave of COVID at the fag end of the last academic session, when the education came to a screeching halt and the alternatives were looked upon to keep the education process rolling. Given the completion of the majority of teaching-learning activities in off-line mode by March 2020 the students were assessed based on the continuous assessment carried out by institutions and students were promoted without examinations. But the session 2020-21 started in the online mode of teaching-learning activities with inherent limitations of lack of equity and access to all. The dreadful second wave of COVID acted like icing on the cake. Consequentially, students appeared to have been dismayed by the policy of offline examination.

Simultaneously, the questionable sanctity of online examinations and uncertainty in holding examinations in offline mode acted as a deterrent for the examination conducting bodies too.

Consequences of examination hesitancy

The capitulation of education regulating bodies to the no-examination impelled for evolving assessment methodologies, with the aptest one being a formative assessment like cumulative estimation based on the weighted average of marks obtained at different previous classes. Unequivocally, for the inconsistently performing students, the new model of assessment cannot be a true indicator of the capabilities possessed by students in the respective class and will not be credible as compared to end-of-course examination outcome practiced in past for that class.

The lesser credibility of marks awarded under such circumstances of no-examination will compel such students for a series of test(s) to put them in order of merit as their marks of respective classes do not speak of their course-specific actual learning and capabilities.

Thence, the students of the class of 2021 may have a life-long notional discriminator of marks without class-specific examination attached to their mark sheets/certificates that may gain prominence after the pandemic passes over.

Unless the academic framework is not put in place for realizing the formative assessment, any loss in the credibility of mark sheets/certificates may have long-term implications of lessening the sanctity of examinations.

The impacts of alternatives worked out as a substitute for end-of-course examination-based results will be evinced on all students, nevertheless, the meritorious ones may feel the greater pinch of it.

Also, the absence of examinations creates a strong perception of these being bootless and emboldens students for skipping the classes which will inevitably converge into lesser competence of so called educated ones.

In addition to this, the education regulators succumbing to the pressure of no examination will set the wrong precedences that could be ingeminated in the future.

Overcoming examination hesitancy

Considering the lack of an alternative worthwhile student learning assessment framework, it is pertinent to brood upon the fast pervading examination hesitancy in the students emanating primarily from their learning insufficiency.

The academics of the country has to collectively ponder upon the following as measures for overcoming examination hesitancy.

- Ensuring adequacy of teaching-learning processes whether in online or offline mode by facilitating the students and teachers with requisite resources suitably so that the challenges posed by the digital divide, socio-economic conditions, etc. do not affect the access and equity in any way.

- Not holding examinations without proper teaching of the complete course and ascertain that no one is deprived of learning opportunities.

- Create, establish, and execute the foolproof digital framework for formative assessment throughout the academic session so that the learning assessment of students is carried out incessantly during teaching and thus make the end-of-course examinations inutile.

- Till the alternative to the present examination-evaluation model is not in place, make the holding of end-of-course examination inexorable.

- Evolve legitimate framework for online examination and assessment for meeting out exigencies with requisite infrastructure.

- The delays in sustaining academic sessions be accommodated by remodeling the academic activities without sacrificing the rigour involved in them.

- Educating the stakeholders about the consequences of no-examinations and counseling students and parents for not pressing the demand of no-examination.

With the examination hesitancy continuing in the second academic session, it is pertinent for the regulators and academic community to contemplate and find the way forward to dissuade all from any thinking to get rid of the end-of-course examinations.

Needless to say that the reluctance of students for appearing in offline mode of end-of-course examinations in the COVID period is not unfounded, but the better alternatives to the no-examination situation can always be worked out without affecting the credibility of mark sheets.

****

CHAPTER XV

Blended Learning in Indian Higher Education: How Feasible is it?

Accolades to University Grants Commission (UGC) for out of the box thinking in allowing the higher education institutions (HEIs) to teach up to 40% syllabus of each course (other than SWAYAM courses) through online mode and remaining 60% of the syllabus in the offline mode along with their examinations in the respective mode. Such a mixed-mode of teaching subjects is referred to as blended learning (BL).

It is the educational practice of combining digital learning tools with more traditional classroom face-to-face teaching with both the student and the teacher physically located in the same space in ideal conditions and extensive use of digital tools. It is pertinent to assess the feasibility of blended learning in Indian higher education.

The concept note circulated in this regard has evoked mixed reactions in the academic community. However, the call for a paradigm shift in teaching pedagogy to BL does not appear unreasonable due to the prevailing circumstances.

Among different reasons for discussions about such pedagogy, the disruption of normal teaching-learning processes on campuses of HEIs for the last two academic sessions and certain aspirations of National Education Policy 2020 happen to be the key ones.

Unequivocally, all of HEIs had partly or fully resorted to online mode to sustain teaching-learning activities during the lockdown, though it has been a very bumpy ride till now. Nevertheless, this has accelerated the thinking for arriving at some appropriate alternatives to such disruptions while attempting to provide ease of access, equity and make it student-centric enriching the quality of education.

Also, the rocketing of digital learning platforms and learning management systems along with the progression of students in the absence of traditional mode of teaching & evaluation has catalyzed the thinking that it is possible to mitigate the role of on-campus teaching-learning processes.

Earlier too, the methodological transformations have been tried for motivating students to build their own learning through flipped classroom and gamification strategies adopted by teachers. But, the reliance on self-learning by students necessitates developing critical thinking, enhanced engagement in the learning process, and cultivating interaction amongst students for mutual development which cannot be accomplished without teachers being adequately trained for practicing the teaching pedagogy they wish to use.

There always exists a gap between theoretically forecasted advantages of the methodological transformations in teaching-learning processes and the actual accrued ones. As a result, the conventional mode of teaching in face-to-face mode has proved to be the most effective one, although any supplementary attempt to enrich it for enabling better learning is praiseworthy.

Now, with the BL under consideration having a predefined proportion of online and offline modes of teaching in each subject is bound to have certain implications. The projected benefits of BL include increased learning skills, greater access to information, improved satisfaction and learning outcomes, and opportunities both to learn with others & to teach others.

These advantages, as envisaged from the blended learning, demand rigorous introspection in the context of the country's socio-economic conditions, preparedness of HEIs, requisite digital infrastructure, student experiences about the online teaching-learning-evaluation in the last two academic sessions, and the public perception on the top of it.

It is worthwhile to note that online teaching-learning has been of interest for more than three decades in HEIs worldwide but such study programs are still not plentiful, ergo, the candid assessment of certain aspects of BL is opportune.

Deterring Digital Divide

As regards BL depending on online processes, it is prudent to be mindful of the fact that the prevailing challenge of the significant digital divide in the country may not allow a sizeable population to be part of online activities unless these are duly facilitated.

Lack of access to poor students and those in locations that are devoid of good internet connectivity will limit the opportunities of collaborating the intellectual endeavours for shared virtual learning across the boundaries.

The student aspirations of flexibility by allowing learning anytime and anywhere, interactivity between students and also with teachers, providing additional digital learning resources, creation of an online community of learners, etc. inevitably require bridging of digital divide at the first hand.

Else, the students from well-off classes will be reaping the benefits of the online activities, and those from poor classes will be mere spectators and get inculcated with frustration.

Availability of learning resources

Since time immemorial, the HEIs have been trying to ensure the availability of learning resources through the enrichment of library facilities. But, the absence of compelling requirements of the thoroughness of study in the classroom and examinations have evinced changes in study pattern.

The ease of availability and open access of generic learning resources digitally has declined the use of library resources by the students.

Consequently, it is imperative to augment the teaching-learning-evaluation processes for ensuring thorough learning. BL may help in achieving the targeted learning levels provided the students are facilitated by the good quality learning resources and teachers make them confront with comprehensive assessment & examination focussing on the holistic learning of respective subject(s).

Training of teachers for increasing the rigour of teaching-learning-evaluation processes is equally important for creating a positive impact of BL.

Virtualization

BL seeks for a predetermined share of online interactions in each subject, meaning thereby that a portion of every subject will be covered in online mode. Contemplating the feasibility of online teaching in each subject raises genuine questions on its rationality, especially in the courses requiring hands-on training. It is arduous to teach such courses online.

Even the mix of face-to-face classes and online classes in laboratory-based subjects like those of science, engineering, technology, medicine, art & design, etc. will not allow students to thrive in complementary virtual interactions. However, supplementing the on-campus classes of HEIs with digital content will definitely be gainful.

Technology integration

BL aims at making learning resources and experiences repeatable, reliable, and reproducible with the use of technology. The technology integration in the conventional teaching pedagogy for making it partially offline and online will levy cost as well as huge human resource engagement over a period of time. A cue can be drawn from the fact that even all HEIs of the country do not have active websites/ portals that are fully functional and free from dead pages to date!

Therefore, envisioning effective technology integration for BL across all HEIs in the country is a delusion. Howbeit, the success of BL in some HEIs will be stellar and should not be misconstrued for being mandated to others without nurturing them for technology integration.

Alongside, the HEIs have to incur huge expenditures for equipping themselves with suitable learning management system (LMS), enterprise resource planning (ERP) software, internet bandwidth of 1-10 Gbps, Wi-fi campus, intranet in campus, computers, data storage systems, smart classrooms, virtual laboratory facilities, studio facility, plagiarism checking software, domain-specific software, teachers & staff training, etc.

Peer learning

The role of cooperative learning amongst students in school classrooms (and afterward in HEIs) has contributed significantly to their overall learning. It is the reticence of students in the formal teaching-learning process that demands peer interaction for mutual learning. The online mode is likely to reduce student participation in the learning process, which means peer learning will have to be made predominant through group activities or in other ways.

Also, special efforts may be required for creating effective provisions for non-verbal interactions like that of the chatroom, gesture buttons, etc. during online teaching.

Offline and online evaluation

In view of the same subject being taught in two modes, the BL may call for online evaluation for the content shared in online mode; and offline evaluation for the content shared in offline mode. Philosophically, there is a rationale behind this. But, the limitations of duly proctored online assessment need to be addressed.

The continuous comprehensive evaluation, open book / closed book examination models, group examinations, viva-voce, presentations, e-portfolio, etc. have been prescribed by UGC as evaluation strategies. Undoubtedly, the evaluation strategies are meaningful but the challenge lies in their execution with integrity.

Obviously, the HEIs intending to introduce BL will be invoking its governance, academic community, students, and supporting staff together for creating the framework to implement it. But utmost care is to be taken to make certain that methodological transformation does not incur any loss to the stipulated class time, fairness of processes, student-centric teaching processes, digital divide, and associated infrastructure support.

It goes without saying that the partial realization of teaching-learning-evaluation processes in online mode will call for the enabling environment as well to achieve the desired objectives of increased student engagement in learning, enhanced teacher and student interaction, responsibility for learning, time management and flexibility, improved student learning outcomes, enhanced institutional reputation, more flexible teaching, and learning environment, more amenable for self and continuous learning, and better opportunities for experiential learning.

Holistic and collective brainstorming across the HEIs is required before exercising the major shift from the conventional face-to-face teaching approach lest BL may have limited cosmetic value.

****

CHAPTER XVI

Remodelling of class 10, 12 assessment calls for utmost care

Accolades to the Central Board of Secondary Education for a candid indication that the cancelling board examinations are not the way forward to handle COVID disruptions. The remodeled assessment framework brought out recently dwells upon the premise that the learning level assessments at classes 10 and 12 are of great relevance and should not be got rid of. It is encouraging for the academic community to witness the regulator evolving strategies to negotiate the situation faced by the country in the event of the third wave of pandemic dislodging the ongoing academic session in the future. The silver lining in this pronouncement of the modified assessment strategy by the board is its timing. Unlike previous academic sessions when the fear psychosis of pandemic panicked the students in class 10 and 12, the board has informed its action plan well in advance to all stakeholders, which will help them study and get assessed accordingly.

The central board has highlighted its continued focus on assessing stipulated learning outcomes by making the examinations competencies and core concepts based, student-centric, transparent, technology-driven, and having advanced provision of alternatives for different future scenarios. On the face of the board's action plan, it appears somewhat similar to the Continuous and Comprehensive Evaluation (CCE) enforced in the country in 2009 as part of the Right to Education. There is no point in pondering upon the reasons for the discontinuance of CCE in 2017 for class 10 board examinations. But, considering the limitations imposed by frequent closure of education institutions due to pandemics since the last two academic sessions, the wisdom calls for exercising formative and summative assessment on the pattern as envisaged in CCE for a reasonably fair assessment.

Indisputably, the educational institutions will have to shoulder the additional burden of creating and practicing the newer continuous assessment tools to capture the continuous learning of their students. However, it is not very difficult in the present time when all concerned are coherently exposed to the use of IT tools and facilities provided in it. The board and education institutions together shall have to be reasonable towards students engulfed in the unequal availability of computers/laptops/smartphones/tablets, internet connectivity, the effectiveness of online teaching, and various socio-economic challenges concerning the students from economically weaker sections and those in remote parts of the country.

With the special scheme of assessment for board examinations of classes 10 and 12 being enforced by the central board, the respective state examination boards will also be under obligation to come up with similar strategies with cosmetic changes suiting their constraints. Therefore, it is prudent on part of the students of respective classes and preceding classes to gear up for getting assessed accordingly. The institutions shall now be assessing their students frequently and the student performance in such assessments cumulatively may affect their overall performance. Hence the alertness of students in classes being held in whatsoever format, self-learning initiatives for seeking knowledge of the subjects taught, will help them in performing well in these periodic assessments which will eventually be contributing to the final assessment outcome compiled by the board.

Unequivocally, the frequent periodic assessment offers ease to students in terms of the reduced domain of assessment which permits them to perform better as compared to the situation in which the domain of assessment is vast. The students getting assessed periodically about their learnings in different portions of the syllabus also ensures the qualitative improvement of learning level assessment as a whole. Under the changed circumstances, the students have to be punctilious to study continually and remain engaged with subjects for proper learning. Students also come to know the outcome of their internal assessments and have an opportunity to improve upon them in the next assessment.

As regards the teachers, extra efforts will be inevitably required from their side for carrying out periodical learning level assessments. The compelling circumstances are likely to be created by the students for learning the subjects properly throughout the period in which the teaching-learning process is carried out. Irrespective of whether the teaching activities are online or offline, the increase in aspiration level of students about their better competencies in the subject domain is bound to exhibit significant improvement in quality of education. Teachers will be accruing the advantage of knowing the extent of thrust required for teaching the relevant portions of the syllabus and can amend their teaching style and rigour.

In exercising the formative and summative assessment together, the board has to meticulously devise the digital framework for capturing student performance. The education institution has to facilitate its teachers for making them creative and fastidious in evolving and executing the assessment strategies with the utmost integrity. The efficacy of the whole process of assessment lies primarily in the institution-level assessment and the prescribed two-term assessments carried out by the board. Given the board functioning remotely for all students enrolled in the institutions affiliated to it uniformly, the rationality of term assessment tools can not be subjected to scrutiny unless some big fallacy is there. However, the institution-level assessment getting executed through different teachers, the scope of variance in assessment method, tools, and its quality can not be ruled out. It is obligatory on the part of the institution to prepare and announce a rational and acceptable evaluation strategy in line with that decided by the board. The transparency in student assessment carried out by the institution is extremely essential to build confidence in the students about the remodeled evaluation strategy in the current academic session.

The reduction in the syllabus for respective classes is also on the anvil in this academic session too like the previous session. The insufficiency of time for holding teaching-learning interactions to complete the earlier prescribed syllabus is the logic put forth. Without arguing in favour or against the syllabus reduction, the alternative of stratification of the syllabus in respect to the rigour required in teaching respective portions could have yielded completeness of learning and no truncation of the syllabus.

Undoubtedly the board has brought forward a contingency plan to handle any exigency due to pandemics, nevertheless, the education institutions have to proactively sensitize their teachers and students for achieving fair assessment outcomes. This warrants the board and institution to set up a suitable assessment framework that has integrity, fairness, and transparency in a time-bound manner so that no student has any doubt about his/her learning level assessment. Concerted efforts are required for sustaining the authenticity, reliability, and validity of the student assessment in board examinations.

****

CHAPTER XVII

Anniversary of NEP 2020: Education needs intensive care

It is time for the country to celebrate the first anniversary since the National Education Policy 2020 (NEP) was announced on 29th July 2020. Chronologically, the years 1968, 1986, and 2020 possess the markers in the form of education policies that have been guiding the mammoth education system of the second most populous nation of the world.

Unequivocally, NEP 2020 is a well-drafted, ambitious, and futuristic document full of promises in line with Sustainable Development Goal No. 4 that calls for Quality Education – Ensure inclusive and equitable quality education and promote life-long learning opportunities for all by 2030. NEP 2020, being the first education policy in the 21st century, exhibits an explicit policy level commitment to developing good human beings capable of rational thought and action, possessing compassion and empathy, courage and resilience, scientific temper and creative imagination, with sound ethical moorings and values.

This is an opportune time to look back at the proclaimed phase-wise implementation of NEP 2020 with effect from August 2020. Undoubtedly, the COVID-19 pandemic has disrupted the functionality of the education system and spoiled the rhythm of educational processes completely since March 2020. But the setting up of the requisite framework for operationalising NEP across the country could have continued undeterred. Without going into the merit of the worthiness of the new bodies detailed under NEP 2020, their procrastinated establishment seeds the perception about the continuance of the existing system for some time in the future. The pace of progress to achieve the envisaged reforms under the new education policy for overcoming the so-called miseries of the existing education system hallucinates the promises. The absence of a crystal clear roadmap for accomplishing the much-hyped milestones of holistic and multidisciplinary education calls for immediate interventions to start replacing the existing education model with the one prescribed in NEP 2020. Targeted attainment of full operation of the transformed education system as per NEP 2020 in the decade of 2030-40 is hardly left with less than a decade now.

With the commencement of a new academic session in offing, the time is ripe for the replacement of the prevailing 10+2 system with the envisioned 5 + 3 + 3 + 4 of school education. The new pedagogical and curricular structure has to start with the foundational level that necessitates early childhood care and education from age of 3 years, but the preparedness is imperceptible. The education policy calls for the holistic development of learners by enhancing essential learning, critical thinking, experiential learning, etc. which needs certain expenditure on creating the enablers for it in Anganwadi centres, school clusters/ complexes, National Assessment Centre, etc. Unquestionably, NEP 2020 eyes upon bringing uniformity in the school education in the public and private sector along with mid-day meal scheme extended to pre-school children above the age of 3 years. But the prevailing notion of private schools and convent schools being better than public schools can be broken only by enriching the quality of public school education and keeping its cost within affordable limits of the bourgeoisie class of the country.

Similarly, the availability of teachers in the requisite number warrants recruitments and their training for upgrading them to meet the expectations of good quality holistic education for all. The amelioration in service management and culture, setting up professional standards, special educators' inclusion, etc. will consume time & funds, and the strategic planning on top of them all. The huge number of vacancies of educators in the public sector institutions hunch the commitment of the concerned towards the provisioning of the ample number of teachers in educational institutions.

NEP 2020 entails major overhaul and reenergizing of the higher education sector starting from the efforts to increase gross enrolment ratio, multidisciplinary education, faculty autonomy, institution autonomy, reorganizing the nature of education institutions, setting up of National Research Foundation for outstanding peer-reviewed research, increasing opportunities for public education, scholarships, online education, infrastructure & learning material for physically challenged, internationalization, etc. The remodelling of higher education governance through "light but tight" regulation by a single regulator inevitably requires a series of alterations in the current functionaries, but the same is inconspicuous. This shall require motivated, energized, and capable faculty members as per the student-teacher ratio requirements. Needless to say that every initiative listed herein has financial implications.

The education system of India is currently having Government financing and Self-financing models for running the educational institutions, of which Government spending has a mega share. National Statistics Office statistics show that the education for classes 1 to 4 has Government funding of 78% while 22 % of the education is self-financed. For classes 5 to 7, this share becomes 82% for Government funding and 18 % for self-financing. For classes 8 to 12, Government funding is 81% & self-financed is 19 %, diploma/certificate level has Government funding of 63% & 37% self-financed, and the graduate and above level has Government funding of 75% & 25% self-financed.

It is evident that there exists a sizeable proportion of the education system that relies on Government support. The budgetary provision for thriving the public-funded education in the country, thus, becomes relevant. Even though NEP 2020 refers to the agonizing fact that the public expenditure on education has not come close to the recommended level of 6% of the GDP as per policies of 1968 and 1992, the current allocation, too, continues to reel in the range of 3 – 4% of the GDP. This insufficiency of financing of education is disquieting at the time when the country, adorned with demographic dividends, is aspiring for holistic and multidisciplinary education ushered through NEP 2020. It is beyond the shadow of a doubt that the new framework of education will bring positive changes in the education system, but the outcome will depend upon the financing of education and conscientious execution of the policy prescriptions in the premeditated timelines, some of which appear insurmountable.

On the commemoration of the first anniversary of NEP 2020, it will be prudent on the part of the regulators to revisit the progress made in the on-ground implementation of provisions of NEP 2020 and reschedule the milestones laid in it, else the disorderliness created through it may disarray the existing education system as well. The predominant disruptions caused by the pandemic and the pragmatic view on the desired transformations ought to be taken into consideration before a realizable road map is relaid.

****

CHAPTER XVIII

Why students are steering away from engineering education in India?

Since time immemorial, Indian parents aspire for quality education and careers for their wards - their children to complete the secondary level of education to become engineers, doctors, lawyers, and chartered accountants among other popular jobs in demand. Every profession requires certain courses to be completed and their demands keep on fluctuating depending upon the availability of job opportunities. A large number of Indian families dream of their children pursuing courses in engineering and technology. However, since the last few years, the country has been witnessing a shift in the aspiration and job demand pattern.

As per the statistics of the All India Council for Technical Education (AICTE), the intake of the undergraduate (UG) and postgraduate (PG) courses of engineering and technology is decreasing every year.

Looking at the intake of UG courses in engineering and technology, it is evident that the UG intake has fallen by 17.5 percent from 15,57,110 in 3,293 Institutions in 2016-17 to 12,84,907 in 2,974 institutions in 2020-21.

Annual fall in UG intake in the academic years 2016-17 to 2017-18 is 5.17 percent, 2017-18 to 2018-19 is 4.87 percent, 2018-19 to 2019-20 is 5.36 percent, and in 2019-20 to 2020-21 is 3.34 percent. This evinces the stark reality that engineering education is losing its sheen.

Similarly, the statistics of PG courses in engineering and technology demonstrate the drastic reduction in intake by

25.12 percent since the 2016-17 academic session when the intake was 1,97,166 in 2,236 institutions which came down to 1,47,594 in 1,861 institutions in 2020-21.

Assessing the annual fall in PG intake shows that it is reduced by 5.62 percent during academic sessions 2016-17 to 2017-18, 2.08 percent during 2017-18 to 2018-19, 7.43 percent during 2018-19 to 2019-20, and the maximum reduction of intake by 12.5 percent is seen during 2019-20 to 2020-21.

The statistics of engineering and technology education point to a looming setback to India which has held pride of being a pioneer in engineering, medicine, arts, music, etc. in ancient times. It is much more concerning at a time when India is looking forward to capitalizing on the demographic dividend and emerging as a five trillion economy.

Although the intakes have been diminishing for the last so many years, still it is not too late to analyze the perceptions of key stakeholders, namely students and parents for arriving at the root cause of the students shifting away from engineering and technology.

Unequivocally, a career in engineering and technology is the ambition of the majority of brilliant students finishing secondary education with science and mathematics subjects. Students' perception is still positive about engineering education. However, certain apprehensions concerning the positioning of engineers in society are evident. All parents eye at available job opportunities and career prospects after engineering education as prosperity and good living are a direct function of earnings.

Thus, the moot question to be answered concerning the students drifting away from engineering education is how will it fetch sustainable livelihood and prosperous life?

Every student completing UG or PG degrees in engineering and technology wishes to get a decent job. Generally, in the present circumstances, the confidence of students seeking admission in the first year of the respective courses gets shattered gradually year by year and touches the lowest ebb by the time they are about to pass out. This is primarily due to the uncertainties creeping in student minds because of the scenario prevailing around in respect to their placements and career prospects.

The options after completion of courses are job in the private sector, job in the public sector, self-employment in own enterprises or entrepreneurship, and higher education and research. For quite some time the private sector jobs are majorly seen in computer and IT-related fields, consulting jobs, service sector jobs, etc. while core engineering sector job opportunities are squeezing. As regards the jobs in the public sector, the fast diminishing number of engineering entries in public sector undertakings and the government sector is quite worrisome.

The Engineering Services Examination conducted by the Union Public Service Commission, New Delhi every year is one of the most coveted options for engineering students of Civil, Electrical, Electronics, and Mechanical engineering. The number of posts for which the recruitment is to be made through this examination as per the UPSC notifications in the last few years shows that the vacancies declined with the progression of time as 609, 440, 588, 581, 495, and 215 in the years 2016, 2017, 2018, 2019, 2020, and 2021 respectively. The number of posts in the prestigious service of engineers in the Government of India getting reduced to two digits for certain disciplines is the real worry among graduating engineers.

There is also a significant number of UG students who intend to pursue PG studies due to their passion for higher education and due to no jobs after a UG degree. The PG intake and UG pass out numbers are 18,22,204 and 7,49,720 respectively for the academic session 2018-19 as per AICTE data which means only 24.3 percent of UG students can seek PG education. These numbers have limited relevance till all UG pass-out students are not getting placed otherwise.

For PG degree holders, the major sector offering employment opportunities happens to be the engineering education sector and R&D establishments. The ongoing incessant diminishing UG intake and closure of institutions worsen the placement opportunities for PG students as teachers. Also, the limited indigenous R&D in the industry does not open ample opportunities for engineers and technologists with higher qualifications.

The sector-wise placement of students from IIT Bombay i.e. the most sought after engineering institute in India shows that the placement offers to its students was 35 percent in 'engineering & technology' followed by 18 percent in 'IT/software', 11 percent in 'analytics', nine percent in 'research and development', 8 per cent in 'finance', 7 per cent in 'çonsulting', 6 per cent in 'services', 3 per cent in 'education', three per cent in 'FMCG', and only 1 per cent in 'public sector undertaking'.

Contemplating the data about the fraction of students placed amongst those aspired for placement, the revelations are not very encouraging. Course-wise placement percentage is 92.13 percent for B Tech, 94.33 percent for B Tech+M Tech dual degree, and 83.43 percent for M Tech. This implies that the cent percent of students who possessed the highest merit at the time of admission could not get placement offers even in the best engineering institution of the country.

Further, as per the Failory report, the large failure of around 90 percent of those venturing into entrepreneurship and startups does not bespeak an invigorating state of affairs. Especially, in a developing economy like that of India, the risk-bearing capabilities, financing, job security, social obligations, enabling surroundings, public perception, etc. deter many from getting into entrepreneurship and startups.

Therefore, the absence of sufficient job opportunities appears to be the sole reason for the lessening inclination of students towards engineering and technology education. This puts onerous responsibility on the government to facilitate the creation of massive employment opportunities. While the regulating body, engineering institutions, and engineering academics should collectively introspect the engineering education from a quality and quantity perspective to make it worthwhile as per the present and future requirements without sacrificing its rigour.

****

CHAPTER XIX

Why India seeks higher education in public sector and school education in private sector?

The Indian education system has a large number of schools, colleges, deemed to be universities, and universities for educating children. Presently, the country meets its educational aspirations through educational institutions in the public and private sectors. With the presence of education offerings in the public sector as well as the private sector, it becomes pertinent to assess the preferences of the education seekers. Let us scrutinize the statistics by segregating education up to class 12 under school education and beyond class 12 as higher education.

School Education

As per the Unified District Information System for Education (UDISE) dashboard 2019-20, there are total 15.1 lakh schools with 26.4 crore students, 96.8 lakh teachers, and 10.3 lakh government schools i.e. in the public sector for catering school education. It is reported that the share of the private sector in school education has grown significantly to nearly 47.5% student enrolments in private schools while the enrolments in public sector schools are declining.

Higher Education

At the same time, higher education is catered through 42343 colleges & 1043 universities as reported by the All India Survey of Higher Education (AISHE) in 2019-20. Out of these, 31,390 colleges, 388 private universities, and 88 private deemed to be universities are in the private sector. In higher education, the majority of colleges are affiliated with public universities, so the share of student enrolment in the public sector is quite large as compared to that in the private sector.

Student Choices

A close observation of the choices of students and parents for seeking education in an institution shows that these are distinctively dichotomous in school education and higher education for the educational institutions in the public sector vis-à-vis the private sector. School education is conspicuously preferred in private sector schools as compared to the schools in the public sector. Whilst, when it comes to seeking higher education, the preference of the institutions in the public sector over the private sector is evident. Unquestionably, the higher education institutions in the private sector are fast emerging as chosen destinations for students in many instances. Even the NIRF ranking of higher education institutions in 2020 shows around 20 percent of private-sector institutions securing their places in the top 100 ranks slab.

Reasoning Student Choices

In general, the education institutions are perceived from their teachers, teaching-learning processes, student accomplishments, curriculum, cost of education, overall ambience, and infrastructure. Be it school education or higher education, the factors affecting student choices for them remain by and large similar.

Introspection of school education points to the fact that public schools are not preferred over private schools on account of insufficiency of teachers, weak teaching-learning processes, weak governance, poor overall ambience, and infrastructure. Thus, despite the available teachers being of good competence, the public sector schools are unable to roll out exemplary student accomplishments. The weaknesses in public sector schools and the growing population are constantly pushing for more schools in the private sector.

A look at the cost of school education in institutions of public and private sectors shows that it is, exorbitantly high in private sector institutions as compared to those in the public sector. Notwithstanding the high cost of education in private sector institutions, the parents yearn for getting their wards admitted to such costly education solely to secure their future. For quite some time the public sector schools are unable to captivate the students from affluent families and are limited to educating the kids from the poor sections of the society that cannot afford it in private schools. Unequivocally, the quality of school education being better in private schools as compared to public schools has created a vicious trap of poor quality in and poor quality out in public schools, however, exceptions are always there. Over some time, this has created a public perception about the better quality of education in private schools and the same is further weakening public school education. But, to educate nearly half of the country's population effectively, the overall education system in public schools needs amelioration.

The public schools outperforming private schools in Delhi offers a cue that public school education can be made comparable to private schools, provided there is a commitment to improving it like that of the Delhi Government.

Interestingly, the large number of higher education institutions (HEIs) in the public sector is perceived to be much better than the private sector HEIs. Obviously, it is the better teaching human resource, teaching-learning processes, enabling learning environment, and infrastructure of public sector HIEs that makes them preferred over private sector HEIs. This preference is also attributed to the glorious accomplishments of students from public sector HEIs along with their low cost of education as compared to the private sector HEIs. The age of public sector HEIs being more than that of private-sector HIEs in the majority of cases also puts them in an advantageous position as the stronger alumni base helps in creating their positive perception. Nonetheless, there are few sought-after private sector HIEs too that have been offering good quality education with all requisite enablers for it.

Given the gross enrolment ratio (GER) in higher education of the country being not comparable to the many developed nations, the NEP 2020 has targeted the attainment of 50 GER by 2035. Undoubtedly, the efforts for increasing GER over since last few decades are responsible for the setting up of new HEIs in the public as well as the private sector. Realising the need of students seeking higher education, the new HEIs in the private sector are establishing themselves as worthy destinations. Now, there are many new private sector HEIs that are performing better than new public sector HEIs and this trend is likely to continue. Primarily, the insufficiency of teachers, inept institutional governance, and inadequate funding & infrastructure of HEIs in the public sector are affecting the quality of education from them. Simultaneously, the focussed and aggressive pace of private-sector HEIs is trying to evolve them as worthwhile education centers, nevertheless, the high cost of education due to their self-financed operation acts as a deterrent for many aspirants with poor socio-economic backgrounds.

Way Forward

It is high time for the educational institutions of the public sector whether in school education or higher education to equip themselves with the adequate number of teachers of good quality, efficient education deliveries, required infrastructure, and enabling environment while retaining their characteristics of offering cheap and accessible education with equity. Although, the NEP 2020 has prescribed for good quality and affordable education with access and equity to all education seekers, but much depends upon the honesty and commitment with which specific initiatives are taken by the education providers.

****

CHAPTER XX

Education system in vicious trap of insufficiency and amotivation of teachers in India

Always a matter of pride to proclaim that India, a nation with demographic dividends, possesses a mammoth education system in the world. Perhaps the country's huge population posits it for such a tag, nevertheless, the gross enrolment ratio (GER) needs improvement to match the access to education as that of the developed nations. For many decades, the country has been focussing on expanding the education system to meet the aspirations of its citizens. As a result, the opening of educational institutions in the public sector as well as in the private sector has brought noticeable improvements in GER. Simultaneously, the concerns about the access, equity, and quality of education offered by these institutions are haunting ubiquitously. Therefore, it is inevitable to consolidate the existing education system for good quality deliveries with equal access to all while increasing the number and capacity of educational institutions well equipped with all enablers of education.

Among major influencers of education, the teacher is the most vital enabler for achieving excellence in education. Inexorably, the key to transforming human lives lies in the wholehearted and committed involvement of teachers in the generation building. Diagnosing the sources of inefficiency in the prevailing education system majorly boils down to insufficiency of teachers along with the lackadaisical attitude of teachers emanating from the treatment meted out to them on differing accounts in educational institutions of both the public sector and private sector.

Educational institutions in public sector

As the vacant posts of teachers are rampant across the education system, the non-availability of a sufficient number of teachers in public sector education institutions is a predicament to another predicament of teaching by the temporary teachers hired on contract or period basis remuneration. Thus, the core process of teaching being carried out by the sizable proportion of temporary teachers reeling under uncertainty of makeshift employment always limits their involvement and commitment towards teaching and evaluation activities. In the context of India, job security matters a lot and such insecurity with the mentoring community affects the quality of education deliveries.

Contemplation of poor compensation to temporary teachers in education institutions affects their self-esteem, difficulty in meeting their livelihood requirements, and always on toes for getting some other secured placement, etc. which mars their overall performance in teaching. At the same time, the instances of regular teachers or permanent teachers simply transferring their responsibilities to temporary teachers and exploiting their presence in the institutions are also not uncommon. This complacency on the part of regular teachers eventually culminates in their exiguous inputs to students.

In the case of regular teachers, the delays in their promotions for career progression resulting in their avolition are predominant. Despite the presence of regulations for time-bound upward movement of teachers subject to the attainment of prescribed performance indicators, and its grant from the date of fulfilling eligibility, the delayed career advancement nucleates the dissatisfaction among teachers. It goes without saying that discontentment among teachers on account of any ground impairs the quality of the education system severely. The timely grant of career advancement motivates the beneficiaries and the benediction of students taught by them. Demotivation and dissatisfaction in teachers on account of whichever reasons get reflected in the loss of efficacy in teaching activities and incurs an intangible loss to the students interacting with such teachers. Essentially, a teacher is an entity that has to teach, mentor, and act as a role model for students at all times, then the lethargic attitude of the teacher even for an iota of duration spoils the quality of deliveries. With the education providers in the private sector coming up fast, the time is ripe to encash the available pool of competent teachers to the best of their capabilities and toil hard for recruiting the meritorious ones as teachers to meet the current teaching needs.

Educational institutions in private sector

Fortunately, the private sector education providers are better compliant with the statutory provisions as far as quantitative fulfillment is concerned. Nonetheless, it goes with the reality that mere fulfillment of the number of teachers, staff, and infrastructure does not build up to good quality in all circumstances. The quality of students, performance by teachers and staff, and the way teaching-learning-evaluation processes are carried out predominantly influences the perspective about the private sector education system.

Talking specifically of the teachers in self-financed private sector institutions, the requisite number of teachers is in place with the inadequacy of senior teachers. The financial compensation made to teachers in self-financed private sector institutions is not up to the mark. The lesser financial compensation is attributed to the scanty availability of funds in such self-financed institutions. However, the grant in aid institutions is much better off as their salary expenditure is borne by the government.

Less than stipulated payment of salary to the teachers creates a grudge of advantage of compulsion being sought from them and sprouts inherent disinterest towards teaching and associated activities which are catalyzed by the sense of job insecurity, hostile, and stringent work environment. Quite often, this all leads to job dissatisfaction and estrangement among teachers in private sector institutions.

The common phenomenon with the teachers of private-sector education system includes, hire and fire system of human resource, exploitation, poor service conditions, insufficient leaves, overworking, lack of time for self-development to become good teachers, lesser respect to teachers by students and parents, drifting of powers from the head of the institution to the promoters/owners of the institution, etc.

Unequivocally, some private sector institutions have demonstrated exemplary performance and are highly preferred in admissions. For instance, the presence of Amrita Vishwa Vidyapeetham – a private sector institution, at 13th rank in the overall ranking among the participating higher education institutions in the NIRF-2021(National Institution Ranking Framework) points towards the serious and significant efforts put in by the private sector education providers to achieve excellence. Another pointer about the unsatiated demand for good education lies in the rush of students to seek admission in such institutions despite the reasonably heavy fee charged from them. Introspection shows that it is the fructification of the adherence to the norms and standards prescribed by the education regulators along with their effective institutional governance and doing much beyond these for administering virtuous education.

Way Forward

Diminishing the quality of education is making a clarion call for targeted interventions that are inevitable to ameliorate the state of affairs related to teachers in educational institutions in the public sector and private sector. The merit centric fair recruitments of teachers with commensurate compensation, creation of an effective framework to ensure their contributions as per prescribed teaching and other responsibilities, enticing human resource policies, inspiring leadership for good governance, requisite teaching-learning infrastructure, and, the sufficiency of financing are critically required to smash the vicious trap of insufficiency and amotivation of teachers disfiguring the education system of the country.

With NEP 2020 (National Education Policy) presenting a very ambitious roadmap for welfare and overall development of teachers, the urgency lies in assessing every education institution redressing the plight of teachers through stopping overworking by teachers, getting rid of contractual teaching, merit centric fair recruitment of teachers as per norms, providing minimum wages, parity in salary pattern, payments as per norms, providing exhilarating governance, creating a congenial working environment for restoring the mental satisfaction of the teachers and bringing in happiness at workplace in general. The panacea for tweaking the education system lies in the motivated and satisfied teachers across the institutions, else the buzzwords of access, equity, and accountability will be ludicrous.

****

CHAPTER XXI

The Great Indian Distressful Examinations: An Introspection

Recent incidents of suicides by the NEET (National Eligibility Entrance Test) aspirants just after the conduction of examination is frightening and paints our education system with skepticism. The loss of life on account of fear of not qualifying in any examination refers to the ultimate state of despair in the child who presumes that it is impossible to pass it. Most importantly, similar unfortunate incidents of medical aspirants losing lives have been observed in the past years too, as 14 deaths were reported in 2020, 7 in 2019, and 11 in 2018. Considering the number of registered students being approximately 1.6 million in 2020, the number of students committing suicide may appear minuscule, but the reasons behind such tendency among young students are vexatious.

Simultaneously, the announcement by National Testing Agency (NTA) to debar certain candidates for alleged malpractices in the Joint Entrance Examination (JEE) 2021 and CBI investigation in it concludes that the stakes are quite high. It is, rather, unfortunate that some people try to grab seats following unethical practices which is highly distressing for those toiling hard to secure a seat by merit.

Sadly, despondency among students is sometimes evinced in those participating in other competitive examinations too. This essentially points to the miserable competency of students who eventually lose hope. It is much more bothering at a time when the country has a huge set up of coaching institutions in parallel to the usual set up of schools for providing secondary education.

However, the coaching does incur huge costs on the students in addition to the normal fees charged by schools. Quite likely, the awfully varying socio-economic conditions may not permit all families to afford 'coaching' for their children. Thence, the children who are unable to get into some coaching due to their inability to bear its cost have to solely depend on the learning they had from the formal school education.

It is worth contemplating that the appearing candidates for every examination whether competitive examinations or regular examinations, can be classified into two broad categories – those 'who take up coaching' and those 'who do not take up coaching'. The apparent reason for the requirement of coaching in addition to regular classes lies in the insufficient learning in the formal education system. This compels the students to make up for their learning deficiencies in order to score well in regular as well as competitive examinations.

Interestingly, whenever the results of any examination are declared in the country, the coaching establishments also issue huge advertisements to unveil the performance of the students enrolled with them. These also include most of the best performers of formal education too. Thus, even the brightest minds joining coaching to secure top ranks in various examinations is unsettling and connotes the complete failure of the education system.

It is worth pondering that when the 'brilliant' ones are unable to achieve their academic goals while relying solely upon formal education, then the 'mediocre' and 'below mediocre' students have to inevitably enter into coaching institutions for meeting out their aspirations. Formal education is simply unable to deliver up to expectations.

Nevertheless, the despicable formal education system monopolizes on account of their recognition by the statutory authorities and the enrolment in them becomes mandatory for all. Consequently, the presence of dummy educational institutions merely for the enrolment of candidates for examination purposes and the mushrooming of coaching institutions preparing them to achieve their targets is quite popular nowadays. Today, various cities like Kota, Delhi, Ranchi, Hyderabad, Chennai, Kanpur, etc. have emerged as coaching hubs with a large number of coaching establishments concerning specific examinations. The economy of these cities is predominantly governed by the coachings over there.

As per a report, the Indian coaching industry is growing tremendously and is likely to become worth $130 billion by 2022. Unequivocally, the scrupulous assessment of the growth of the coaching industry pans out to the unworthiness of the formal education system. The diminishing sheen of education institutions in the rising glow of coaching is enticing students toward them. It calls for honest introspection by the academics, even though this has been a concerning issue for quite some time.

Undoubtedly, the examinations are meant for assessing the knowledge, its application, skill, and aptitude irrespective of the nature of the examination, whether its class examination or competitive examination. Quite likely, the exodus of students from the classes in the formal education system to coaching classes is the sequelae of the poor quality of teaching, failure in understanding concepts, lesser care of student learning, absence of doubt removal opportunities, absence of hands-on to complex problem solving, inability to teach as per the latest trends in competitive examinations, slow pace of teaching, etc.

Contrary to this, the coachings allure candidates because of their customized tutoring to suit the specific requirements of scoring well in the examinations.

Unfortunately, the limited focus of coaching towards ensuring good scores pushes the unexpurgated learning to the backseat as the attainment of the end goal is also the priority of students and their families. Howbeit, the purpose of education gets defeated in the absence of thrust on holistic learning of the subjects taught. The limited learning in coaching is aimed to only succeed in certain examination(s) which may have severe implications in the future.

Without any prejudice to the coaching in the country, whether online or offline, it is imperative to track down the reasons for students shifting away from the formal education system towards coaching. It goes without saying that improving the worthiness of formal education will strengthen the knowledge and competence of its students in general. This will automatically resolve the problems of deprivation of financially weak students from coaching as these will become redundant.

Concomitantly, academics should ponder upon the pattern of the examinations so that the processes become reasonably foolproof. Bristling at the recent malpractices, the vulnerability to malpractices in computer-based multiple sessions of the same examination calls for suitable changes in the methodology. Similarly, the examinations being held only once a year limit the chances for examinees, but the vulnerability of examinations to unfair practices gets curtailed. Also, the normalization of marks secured by candidates in multiple sessions, the normalization of multiple sets of question papers, and preparing the inter-se-merit based on multiple sessions always have variances for different candidates.

It should be understood that every candidate will have different perceptions about the same question; it being simple, moderate, difficult, or the most difficult. This means that the qualitative exercise of moderation and quantitative exercise of normalization together cannot supersede the quality of the merit list prepared on the basis of a single examination across the country as done earlier. Moreover, the objective nature of questions is only good for competitive examinations where the merit list preparation based on the candidates' knowledge is the primary objective. However, the subjective questions in regular class examinations should not be substituted by objective-type questions for assessing the learning level of students.

Allaying the fear of failure in any examination is urgently required across the country and at all levels of education. The education system should strategize to avert the fear psychosis in students in respect to any examination. The examination is not the end of the road. Instead, it is an opportunity of knowing the individual's capabilities even through failure and move on to the other possible avenues for a successful life.

Summarily, holistic improvement in the quality of primary education and secondary education holds the key to keeping students away from any distress. Such enhanced learning of students will also pave the way to make coaching institutions redundant.

Concerted efforts are required to create an all-inclusive education culture capable of meeting the contemporary expectations of all examinations. The sole dependence of students on the formal education system should be in focus for transforming the education processes, else the prominence of coaching institutions will continue burdening society with the additional cost of education which could be out of reach for many and depress students from such families or the weaker ones losing their life.

****

CHAPTER XXII

Test Culture in India: Boon or Bane

Holding tests for assessing the suitability of anyone for a particular purpose is the most prevalent practice in India. Here the word test refers to the assessment tools other than the routine examinations in the formal education system.

For everything starting from seeking admission in the education system to securing a job, these tests keep on bothering. At times, after passing certain classes and possessing the certificate, diploma, degrees, etc. it is felt that repeated testing questions the very sanctity of the regular class examinations held for award of certificates, diplomas, or degrees. Unequivocally, subjecting individuals to testing for similar capabilities as carried out by the formal education system for the award of a particular certificate, diploma, degree, etc. raises doubts on the credibility of the teaching-learning-examination-evaluation processes. The moot point is the trustworthiness of the marks awarded to anyone based on examinations conducted by a particular Board, Institution, University, etc.

For many decades now, frequent concerns about the poor employability of students, their skill sets, and competencies have been raised and discussions buzz around about the modalities of the corrections to improve the learner capabilities. But, the situation does not seem to improve.

With the size of the education system growing gradually for attaining the higher gross enrolment ratios at every level, the precarious education system is endangering the lives of a large number of individuals who proudly display the certificates but are unable to prove their corresponding worth.

Who is to be questioned for it? whether institution granting certificate or the student?

Indisputably, no one can doubt the innocence of the students seeking admission in the first class of their formal education process, maybe at the pre-primary level or primary level. This means the innocent ones getting into the formal education process are either not provided ample opportunities to learn and perform well or the students themselves are circumstantially coerced for not being able to do so due to the poor socio-economic conditions of their families.

Eventually, the children grow biologically, as well as class up-gradation academically devoid of commensurate growth in their capabilities. The inculcation of learning deficiencies at the school level has a cascading effect and vitiates the quality of the whole education process and learning outcomes. Consequentially whenever the assessment of capabilities of an individual is to be done, the assessors observe competency gaps and find the education credentials incongruous. As a result, the only available way out is to hold a test and re-assess the learning levels. Tests for opening every future door are tempting students to reorient their studies to target the respective test instead of upgrading themselves conforming to the respective level of formal education. Tests are catalyzing students for preparing in a limited domain and defeat the purpose of formal education. It goes without saying that the credible examination-evaluation processes and sacrosanct grades awarded based on them will eschew the frequent learning assessment tests.

Ailing Education providers

Currently, the Indian education providers at the primary, secondary, and tertiary levels are either in the public sector or in the private sector. However, there are examination boards in control of public authority for terminal examinations of primary and secondary levels of education. The tertiary education system has a sizeable number of private higher education institutions (HEIs) in the form of Universities or deemed to be universities that are statutorily entrusted with the authority to issue degrees based on their examination-evaluation system very similar to the public sector Universities and Institutions. Nevertheless, the broader framework of imparting higher education is prescribed by the regulating bodies in control of the public authorities, but the micromanagement of teaching-learning-examination-evaluation processes is carried out by the HEIs themselves. Therefore, HEIs are responsible for the credibility of degree certificates from the adequacy of learning level quantification perspective.

Among the primary and secondary level education providers, the public sector institutions have slid below the private sector education providers for the sole reason of the quality of academic processes carried out by them. The instances of poor quality teaching in government-controlled primary & secondary schools are ubiquitous, for which teachers and enabling factors are jointly responsible. In most cases, the contractual teaching in such institutions on low wages is unable to keep them motivated enough to effectively nurture the children taught by them. Also, the poor governance of public sector institutions worsens the situation and affects the public perception about them. This has culminated in the mass demand for primary and secondary education in private schools, where too the quality of education is not up to the mark in the majority of instances despite over-regulation and stricter governance based on performance. Again the meager compensation to teachers, their inadequate quality, and job insecurity diminish their motivation and lessen the prospects of better quality education deliveries in spite of student success linked career prospects of teachers.

The shift in focus from learning and seeking knowledge among learners can also be attributed to their myopic aim of merely getting through with good performance in entrance tests for certain career courses. The reduced interest of students in formal education also makes the education providers complacent in imparting education. Thus, it is not the teachers alone to be blamed for the meshy state of the formal education system which fails in examining students credibly.

The examining boards quantifying the learning outcome in the form of student grades are not accepted at face value. The pattern of examination requires reworking for assessing knowledge to align the education system for updating and training young minds accordingly. Circumstances are to be created for the students to get motivated and learn holistically.

Coachings as spoilers

The country is witnessing tutoring for every test whether it is for admission in higher classes or employment. The insufficient capacity addition in the schools/colleges/universities is prompting students to resort to getting trained specially for cracking particular tests in coaching institutions. Presence of coaching as an option to overcome the gaps induce students to rely more on it rather than the formal education providers.

Imagine if there is a complete absence of coaching, then the students will be persuading their teachers and institutions for ensuring that teaching-learning processes are apposite to meet the forthcoming challenges. Undeniably, the coaching establishments are doing a commendable job of taking care of student requirements in limited bandwidth of specific test requirements, but the same is engendering the lackadaisical approach in all enablers of the formal education system and the absence of balanced learning is degrading the overall potential of students.

Role of Regulators

Regulating bodies in the education system of the country are rarely inclined to delve into the regular teaching-learning activities. Their role is primarily confined to according sanctions to the institutions, courses, programmes, standard-setting, and creation of a model framework for the functioning of institutions. The pointers responsible for assessing the institutions for their sustenance have no bearing on the credibility of education offered by them. Moreover, it is not their job to do micromanagement of the institutions but they need to devise a mechanism for mandating the students and institutions together to improve the learning levels and abilities of students so that the terminal examination outcome helps in getting rid of multiple tests for similar kind of assessments. Let the marks obtained be used for all purposes of assessing students which may require moderation in view of slight variations from board to board and university to university. The recent pronouncement of the All India Council for Technical Education (AICTE) for holding tests for mid-course assessment of the learning levels and employability of engineering and management students studying in institutes approved by it is pointing towards regulator jumping into the in-course assessment of student learning. Such interventions may not serve the purpose as it is the institution that has to take a call and improve the overall education delivery and make their assessment tools foolproof and realistic indicators. Mid-course assessments are already done by the institutions through their routine examinations and the same require strengthening.

The poor reliability of scores obtained in terminal examinations is leading to re-testing of students for gauging their proficiencies and unless the terminal examination assessment of examining boards, Universities, and Institutions becomes credible, it is not possible to get rid of tests-tests-tests.

****

CHAPTER XXIII

Equitable and Accessible Education in COVID-hit India: A Mirage?

The Supreme Court of India has raised serious concerns on the issue of the digital divide in the context of online education in SLP no. 4351/2021 on 08th October 2021. Taking cognizance of the deprivation of education to the children belonging to poor families due to the cost of online education, the court exhorts to make online education accessible to all with equity. The three-judge bench has explicitly observed the consequences of the digital divide upon the children belonging to Economically Weaker Sections (EWS) & Disadvantaged Groups (DG). These children either dropped out or could not pursue education because of their inability to afford internet access and computer, smartphone, laptop, etc., without which online education is not possible.

The Supreme Court order is full of indignation on the account of online education being confined to the children of the families that can afford it. This has questioned the whole orchestration of online education and the trumpeted '*sabka saath, sabka vikaas, sabka vishwas*'.

Faux pas of Academics

The court has graciously incriminated the system for the deprivation of destitute pupils from the new normal of education i.e. online mode. It is very unfortunate on the part of the academic community and academic governance for not being pragmatic enough in treating their students alike with respect to offering learning opportunities.

Undoubtedly, few academics were disquieted with the way online education started rolling in the country without consideration of the severe digital divide and hugely varying socio-economic conditions. Since the spread of the pandemic and the closure of educational institutions, there are numerous writings in the public domain that demonstrate the worries of the academic community about unequal access to online education.

Academic governance has to introspect and find answers to whether respective institutions were equipped for starting online education when it was mooted. The IT facilities for the preparation of digital learning material, the mechanism for its dissemination, and the online teaching facilities available to the teachers were also not assessed.

The educational institution must do soul searching as to why did they not take feedback about the feasibility of online teaching mode before kicking it off. Juxtaposing Indian socio-economic conditions with the education model of the nations having significantly strong IT infrastructure and much better capabilities as compared to India is irrational.

Let us not lose sight of the fact that a large number of our education providers do not have their digital presence. But all institutions plunged into online education activities ignoring the extent of facilities available with their students and teachers. Surely, the digital mode of interaction is not a handicap for those from well-off families. Nevertheless, the penury coercing the poor to the extent of leaving the mainstream education has not only flouted the constitutional provisions regarding the right to education but also forbidden the talented ones to chip in for the good of humanity and civilization.

Society trusts every act of teachers as the best for their students and any irresponsible action affects the future generations while also diminishing their sheen. Cardinally, the teachers should exalt the student interests and indiscriminately safeguard equitable access to learning opportunities for all. The court has propitiously triggered a discourse on the contribution of much-hyped online education. Unequivocally, students are bearing the brunt of this mode of teaching-learning-examination-evaluation process. Taking care of the voids created by limitations of the online mode being forsaken at the mercy of someone is not in the larger interest of society.

Digital Divide

Presently, the reach of the internet in India is not uniform across its whole territory. The scanty or no electricity is also another impediment to the serviceability of electricity-run IT gadgets across the country. International Telecommunication Union had earlier estimated that by the end of 2019 more than 51% of the global population will be using the internet. While in India, as per the reply to a question in the Parliament, the Telecom Statistics India – 2019 report states that there are 25.36% and 97.94% internet users in rural and urban India, respectively, among the total 636.73 million internet subscribers.

The internet subscribers in rural and urban areas are 227.01 and 409.72 million, respectively. National Sample Survey Office (NSSO) reports about the presence of a desktop/laptop/tablet/computer in one in every ten households in India.

National Broadband Mission, started on 17th December 2019, targets to provide every Indian village with a broadband internet facility by 2022. This will take care of the digital divide arising out of infrastructure deficiency. But special efforts of providing IT gadgets with enablers for internet access to poor children will overcome the challenge posed by the lack of IT gadgets and internet access due to the weak economic conditions of the families.

Way Forward

Going by the present scenario, it is discernible that online education has been progressing undeterred without much concern for those unable to take it. Thence the loss of learning opportunities has already occurred. A large number of impoverished ones had to leave the online education system for want of IT resources. At the same time, the instances of loss of job of the earning members in the families have incapacitated a sizeable number to afford the education expenses of their children.

Hitherto, there are two types of children who could not afford online education, either due to the unavailability of internet services in their region or due to the unavailability of IT gadgets for accessing it. Strategizing the bridging of the digital divide calls for huge investment for setting up internet infrastructure and providing the requisite equipment free to learners for enabling them to join online education.

Offering free education to children of families in financial hardships as also envisaged by the statutory provision of the Right to Education may help. Also, the concerted efforts for providing learning opportunities in offline mode to those who suffered learning loss because of online education may help the deprived ones in coming back to mainstream education and overcoming knowledge gaps.

In the meantime, getting rid of online education and resorting to offline education having face-to-face learning following prescribed pandemic protocols shall help to make it accessible to the majority of children. In a country with around 1.3 billion population of varying economic stature, it is inevitable to holistically assess the feasibility of the so-called new normal of education, i.e., online education and blended mode of education before starting it. Further, involving all stakeholders, including teachers, students, parents, and regulators before taking all acceptable decisions on the methodology of imparting education should become the thumb rule to avoid any grudges in any part of the society.

****

CHAPTER XXIV

Dissecting selection of leadership in higher education institutions

Unequivocally, the growth in the number of Universities has triggered the conflict between the quality and quantity at all levels in academics. The uncalled-for interferences, biases, and sacrifice of merit in the process of recruitments of the head of higher education institutions (HEIs) like Vice-Chancellors and Directors have brought down the sheen. Umpteen number of Vice-Chancellors are reported to be involved in financial, academic, and administrative irregularities from time to time. Consequentially, HEIs are doomed in misgovernance and innocent students face the brunt. The non-inspiring leadership of HEIs is primarily responsible for their inability to command respect among the teachers and students of the respective institution which plunges the institution into mediocrity. Messy higher education is endangering the intellectual prowess of the country blessed with the demographic dividend. Nevertheless, the same has been part of the discourse in academics and government for quite some time, but the amelioration is not perceptible. The challenge posed by tendentious leadership in HEIs entails the earliest fixing of what is wrong in picking up academic leadership, especially in public sector HEIs holding a larger share in higher education.

Questionable identification of persons

Despite all efforts made by regulating bodies from time to time, the appointment of the head of HEIs in the public sector has been vexatious. The quality of leadership can be assessed from the findings of a committee reported in 2019 by Times News Network stating that 75 percent of VCs are unfit to hold the post. For example, the alleged involvement of academic leadership in unethical practices of academics, plagiarism, taking bribes for granting favours, giving bribes to get the position, misconduct, etc. are ubiquitous. Disclosure of certain corruption in the appointment of Vice-Chancellors by one of the Chancellor puts rest to all speculations. There are ample shreds of evidence of contentious identification of persons with sullied and modest credentials Often the litigations are witnessed against leadership and culminate into their termination or continuing judicial probe or go beyond the tenure. Undoubtedly, such polemical cases corroborate the serious predicament in designating leadership in HEIs.

The compromises made in identifying persons to lead academics are proved by the prima facie evidence of their misdeeds or from their tendering resignations before completion of tenure or the appointing authority sacking / relieving them. Questioned integrities of the heads of HEIs, howsoever minuscule their number is, pose a bigger threat and are completely unacceptable in the educational institutions that preach quality, integrity, and honesty to their students.

Dwindling brilliance in appointment

University Grants Commission (UGC) has norms for the appointment of Vice-Chancellors. However, the appointments made in violation of these are often seen around with the criteria of deciding excellence being loaded with selectivity.

Historically, the persons appointed as head of HEIs used to be the persons of the highest integrity and reputed experts. Best academics were approached to accept the responsibility of leading a particular HEI and the individuals rushing for the posts were nearly absent.

Nowadays, the old practice of picking individuals through the Search Committee has been substituted through the Search cum Selection Committee (SSC) and formal public notification.

The lowering of benchmark parameters for identifying the suitability of individuals due to various considerations has abated the dignity of academic leadership. The compromises made in selecting the mediocre individuals as academic heads have emboldened the members of the academic fraternity to aspire for heading HEIs even without having worthy credentials and accomplishments.

Consequently, the number of applications received against the advertisement of the post of Vice-Chancellor has grown up significantly. Reference is also made to the advertisements for the post of Vice-Chancellor in two Universities of Haryana in which the candidates are required to pay Rs.2000/- (Rs.500/- for SC/ST candidates of Haryana only). This is disgraceful to the respective University and demeans the prestige of the position which once used to be filled by invitation as per the prudence of the Search Committee and the Chancellor. It is also in stark contrast to the practices followed for the apex position appointments in academics or other organizations.

Reasoning the ailing leadership

While attempting to reason the ailing leadership, the focus is upon the whole process starting from preparation of panel to finalization by the competent authority. The vested interests of individuals in seeking the coveted positions have yielded a paradigm shift in criteria for screening, preparing a panel of few names, and the process of convergence on one name.

Apparent reasons are the formation of a pliable search-cum-selection committee with the members having questionable integrity, vested interests, conflict of interests, lack of rigour, arbitrariness in describing merit, and insufficient diligence by the SSC.

Quite often the quid pro quo between the members of SSC and the aspirant is talked of in which SSC member buttressing certain name gets entitled to similar help by the propped one in future.

Instances of unethical considerations & obligations between the candidate and those pushing the candidature, selectivity in the interpretation of provisions as suited to the particular candidate by the appointing authority, misuse of proximity to the concerned offices by the incumbent Vice-Chancellors in managing their further appointments, etc. are also murmured.

Way forward

The quality of leadership in HEIs is a cornerstone in improvising the education in the particular HEI, and the sacrifices of merit and competence of eligible ones mar the institution in particular and the whole education system in general. The losing radiance of HEI leadership eventually calls for immediate correction.

Steadfast adherence to the prescribed provisions and constitution of SSC with the persons of impeccable integrity will nucleate the probity in the process and rule out the possibility of quid pro quo.

Further, the selection proceedings should be solely proforma-based with weighted considerations to accomplishments as the interview infuses subjectivity. Obligating SSC for recording the quantitative and qualitative merit behind picking up respective candidates in the recommended panel will impel conscious volition along with the process becoming transparent, credible, and free from undue influences. For accruing advantage of the experience of persons completing terms as head of HEIs in strengthening their parent HEIs, the maximum leave admissibility in a row can be restricted which shall bring in a diversity of individuals and variety of thoughts in academic governance. Best practices of the corporate sector in identifying the leadership should be followed for timely appointment of new Vice-Chancellor or Director well before completion of tenure.

Truly speaking, the academic appointments have to demonstrate utmost integrity, fairness, and transparency. Unfortunately, the wiled appointment of persons with a chequered academic and administrative history as the head of HEIs germinates insouciance in the good academicians which could be devastating. It is ineluctable for the Government and the regulators to make the process of appointment of academic heads solely merit-centric.

****

CHAPTER XXV

Metamorphosing Industry 4.0 to Industry 5.0 Requires Engineers From All Domains

Year by year, engineering admissions are witnessing a peculiar drift of students towards courses in computer science, information technology, and allied disciplines. This has culminated in the springing of programs offering degrees in computer-related disciplines with a focus on software engineering, artificial intelligence, data science, cloud computing, etc.

There are numerous instances of technical institutions shutting down traditional engineering disciplines of Civil, Electrical, Mechanical, etc. due to fewer takers for them. Most of these institutions have increased their intake in computer science and floated similarly placed programs in related disciplines which have current demand. Nevertheless, the speculations of future technical manpower demand after 3-4 years should rely on the prospective changes in industry & society.

Unequivocally, computers and information technology have revolutionized present-day life, but this all has been possible because of the availability of the infrastructure, manufacturing technologies, and framework required for facilitating the same.

Given the relevance of traditional disciplines of engineering for sustaining and advancing the technologies, it is germane to introspect the implications of the prevailing trend in engineering admissions, especially at a time when the fifth industrial revolution (termed industry 5.0) is in offing.

Aspiring students and their guardians must assess the forthcoming scenario of technical human resource requirements in metamorphosing industry which shall require all engineers and technologists.

Further, the mass exodus of meritorious students to one particular discipline of engineering will build up to a skewed competency across the technological world which may be deleterious for sustenance and the forward march of civilization. The workforce from across subject disciplines has to inevitably have brilliance, so that synergy contributes to the judicious application of science and technology in maintaining, innovating, and developing solutions for industrial and economic development.

Industry 4.0

The contemplation of the industrial revolutions in the past and the ongoing fourth revolution points to the digital transformations. Undoubtedly, the cyber-physical systems led productivity improvement, digital services, e-commerce, artificial intelligence (AI), etc. along with ease of handling resulted in the growth of employment opportunities for computer and IT professionals with the presence of adequate technical personnel from other disciplines to facilitate the technology-driven Industry 4.0.

The present era of the industrial revolution focuses more on digitalization and AI-driven technologies for enhancing flexibility in production and efficiency. These transformations in workplaces, learning throughout life, team working, newer career prospects, and knowledge management led to the creation of the social-technical system.

The mass employability of engineering graduates, irrespective of their discipline in the IT sector, became a godsend as it seeded the collapsing of the rigid boundaries between disciplines. However, this sector is unable to offer employment opportunities to all, and engineering graduates from traditional disciplines are seen wandering in search of jobs for long. This creates a perception of fewer jobs for engineers from traditional disciplines as compared to computer science and related professionals, which is, in fact true.

But, the perennial demand of expanding, removal of obsolescence, and sustaining civil infrastructure, electricity, machines, and equipment, etc., along with setting up new industries to meet the contemporary requirement entails the presence of a large number of engineers from all disciplines in times to come.

Industry 5.0

The impending fifth industrial revolution – Industry 5.0 – is value-driven and envisages exploiting human creativity for getting efficient and intelligent machines for optimal resource utilization and effective manufacturing solutions to increase production and customizing products spontaneously. The core values of industry 5.0 being human centricity, sustainability, and resilience are complementary to practices of Industry 4.0 with economic and societal considerations.

The ensuing intelligent healthcare, modern biotechnology, cloud manufacturing, supply chain management, manufacturing production, edge computing, digital twins, robots, internet of things, blockchain, networks of 5G – 6G, etc. necessitate engineers & technologists from all disciplines.

The aim is to engage the industry in realizing prosperity beyond jobs and growth through production processes having a focus on well being of human resources.

The key enabling technologies in Industry 5.0 as per the results of a workshop on Enabling Technologies for Industry 5.0 with Europe's technology leaders 2020 of European Commission, Directorate-General for Research and Innovation are listed as below ;

- Individualized human-machine interaction technologies that interconnect and combine the strengths of humans and machines.
- Bio-inspired technologies and smart materials that allow materials with embedded sensors and enhanced features while being recyclable.
- Digital Twins and simulation to model entire systems.
- Data transmission, storage, and analysis technologies that are able to handle data and system interoperability.
- Artificial Intelligence to detect, for example, causalities in complex, dynamic systems, leading to actionable intelligence.
- Technologies for energy efficiency, renewables, storage, and autonomy.

It pertinently calls for the apposite presence of all engineers, technologists, and scientists to achieve the envisioned augmentation of research and innovation support to industry for ensuring its long-term smart service to humanity.

Thence, the engineering aspirants must choose discipline as per their passion and interest, instead of rushing only for a few computer science & engineering-related disciplines. Moreover, the future lies in the application of digital know-how to the existing and upcoming systems from various domains.

Policy Facilitation

Above all, the National Education Policy 2020 prescribes multidisciplinary education so that the compartmentalization of education does not hinder in fulfilling the aspirations of anyone. Remodeling engineering education in the light of NEP 2020 with the concept of minor and major specializations will enable students to get professionally equipped in more than one discipline. The cross-fertilization of a variety of concepts may call for technical professionals possessing a broader range of expertise which is enabled by the new policy framework. This enjoins technical professionals from every engineering discipline with vital competencies, and the same can not be merely taken care of by computer and IT-related professionals alone.

The curriculum for engineering graduates belonging to non-computer disciplines needs reorienting for enhancing digital competencies in their specific domains. This will be better met with brilliant minds landing into traditional disciplines too, else deficient capabilities of such core engineering professionals may end up hampering technological upgradation and sustainable developments.

Also, employment opportunities being the biggest push factor in choosing the engineering discipline at graduation level, it is imminent to create ample opportunities for placement of technical professionals from traditional disciplines and maintain the balance of intellectual capabilities across engineering and technology disciplines before it is late. Regulating bodies and academics must formulate an explicit road map for the development of suitably trained manpower ranging from skilled workers to highly qualified engineers, technologists, and scientists so that there is no shortage of technical personnel in respective domains. History shows that running crash programmes to train personnel for meeting emergent demands is time-consuming, costly, and adversely affects research & development. Time is ripe to analyze, forecast, and disseminate the information about the sectorial/specialized manpower requirement to the public at large and facilitate youth in selecting courses for study accordingly.

****

CHAPTER XXVI

Money Matters in Higher Education

The Supreme Court's direction to IIT Bombay for granting admission to a student who was denied admission due to his inability to pay fees must be an eye-opener to the regulators. Apex Court has exercised powers under Article 142 and passed the order for creating a seat to admit him and called such instance of denying admission as 'great travesty of justice because it happened despite the student's attempt to pay fees. The seriousness in hearing a genuine case with a humanitarian approach by the top Court of the country deserves acclamation. The issue is not limited to the mere grant of admission to one destitute student, who could approach the Supreme Court after being unheard in the Bombay High Court. Also, such relief may not eventuate in all such cases of impoverished deprivation.

In one more petition on similar deprivation of a financially weak student from admission in IIT BHU, the Allahabad High Court Judge namely Justice Dinesh Kumar Singh ordered for creation of a supernumerary seat to admit the said student and voluntarily paid her fees himself.

This nucleates serious thinking on penury offsetting the merit of children who are termed the future. This is astounding at a time when a lot of hype is created around access and equity in education. Does it not germinate a few basic questions like, 'how many talented students discontinue education on account of financial constraints?', 'how easy to get financial support in continuing education?', and 'are educational institutions capable of tapping talented students or merely operating mechanically to grant admissions following stereotyped format?'. Whatsoever may be the answer to these, the financial incapacitation of students leading to their dropping out of the formal education system is not ruled out. Sometimes, this happens even before the commencement of their journey in the certain course(s) or leaving it in between and moving on for some job to run livelihood of the family.

As per a survey of the National Statistical Office (NSO), one out of every eight students enrolled in school or college drop out of the education system before completing their education in India. This has also emerged as a serious concern in the National Education Policy (NEP) 2020 and measures like reintegration by aligning the practical experience of dropout with the relevant level of the National Skills Qualifications Framework to facilitate mobility across 'general' and vocational education is prescribed therein.

With the gross enrolment ratio in higher education being slightly more than 26.29 for boys and 26.36 for girls, the lack of access to higher education is undeniable. In response to certain questions in parliament, the ministry has informed about falling dropout rates in IITs, IIMs, and other higher education institutions, which points to amelioration through student counseling, mentorship, and peer-assisted learning. However, poverty-stricken students failing to seek admission in a particular programme due to non-deposition of fees is highly worrisome and not coming into the glare. In most of these situations, students consider it as their destiny and remain deprived of opportunities. The moot point is that the availability of money for pursuing the dream of any child at the time of need depends on the financial health of the respective family and the child is not at fault for indigence.

These two instances of court interventions in facilitating admission in professional courses in the prestigious institutions of the country in the 2021-22 session sufficiently cue that the proclamations of access and equity are far from realities at ground zero.

Philosophically, the abilities and competence of anyone cannot be linked to their monetary strength and the money should never become a deterrent in capitalizing on the best brains for being trained to contribute for the good of humanity. One cannot foresee the potential of any child at the time of starting study in some course, nevertheless the loss of opportunity to study further to anyone could incur an irreparable loss as everyone has unique and unparalleled specialties & capabilities.

Undoubtedly, the Government has made enormous provisions for a tuition fee waiver, scholarships, and subsidized education to poor children from all cross-sections of society. But sometimes the extreme poverty and social conditions may make it impossible for students to be able to get admitted into a course in time and seek these advantages.

Looking at the other possible remedy for meeting out deficient financial resources to study further, bank finance comes to mind immediately. Still the process of getting bank funds could be quite cumbersome for those who find certain enablers for bank loans being not amenable to them procedurally. The bank loaning process needs reworking for impecunious students. In nutshell, the pauperized socio-economic conditions predominate the process of securing funds from different means, and there exists no remedy for battening socio-economic conditions. Therefore, the issue of any student getting deprived of the opportunity to study calls for honest introspection and finding a well-reasoned strategy to negotiate occasions of individual losing opportunity to study as per his/her competence on the want of money.

With the access to higher education being in public and private sector both, the former being public-funded type has greater responsibility in provisioning higher education to all deserving ones. The private sector institutions being self-financed type must also ponder upon keeping access to higher education for few such financially weak but talented students under their philanthropic initiatives.

Unequivocally, the collective efforts of the Government, regulators and educational institutions will be able to catch hold of the best talents in educational programmes and nurture them with the best quality education, skills, and competencies so that every young mind can contribute for good of humanity at large. It may not be possible for every needy student to approach Court and seek remedy for the problems emanating out of lack of money with them. Also, India's demographic dividend compels us to delve into all such poverty-centric socio-economic challenges and circumvent them through suitably so that the youth power can be best used for sustainable development and prosperity.

****

CHAPTER XXVII

Corruption breeds corruption and education is no exception

Corruption is a vicious loop and its nucleation engulfs all elements involved in the respective system and its processes sequentially over a while. Since time immemorial, the misuse of the authority vested with an individual or group of individuals have been a matter of concern and witnessed in various forms not limited to the bribery, cronyism, dereliction of duties, financial embezzlement, extortion, graft, influencing, lobbying, nepotism, parochialism, patronizing, etc.

For quite some time the concerns regarding the deteriorating perception about India's education system and shreds of its' fallible integrity are creating a buzz around.

Contemplation shows frequent incidents of question paper leakage in certain school examination boards, University examinations, admission tests to different courses, teacher recruitment tests, etc. Similarly, the instances of nepotism, illegal gratification, forgery in documents, plagiarism, and fraud in teacher recruitment and admissions are not rare nowadays.

On top of everything, the shocking revelations about the alleged use of unfair practices and disregard of merit in selecting academic leadership are vexatious. These uncalled-for manifestations are usually driven by either explicit/implicit monetary transactions or attempts to favour someone out of turn. But the occurrence of even an iota of such iniquitous practices in the supposedly sacrosanct education system and allied processes are disquieting because it daresay the ailing processes of nurturing innocent minds into responsible human beings.

The implications of unethical corrupt practices in education and allied processes affect the standpoint of students about the sanctity of teaching-learning-evaluation processes and the teachers, officers, and staff in the institutions of their study. Disrespect to merit at any stage culminates in the vitiation of the whole education system and the products rolled out from them.

Compromising merit in recruitments

Setting aside competence at the time of recruitment of teachers in schools due to any consideration will result in recruitment of sub-standard teachers which will cause declension of the education quality by lowering the benchmarks and rigour levels suiting constellation of such teachers. Ultimately, the standard of education goes down and the quality of educated ones will be inferior to the past thresholds.

The poor quality of students coming out from school education becomes inferior quality feed for higher education and their inherent limitations in terms of learning gaps enervate the possibility of being not educated with thoroughness and thus lower the quality of higher education too. Though it will create a pool of educated individuals but with deficient quality often baptized as unemployable graduates or postgraduates.

Also, disregarding academic merit in identifying people for academic leadership roles on account of different biases and gratifications has very serious repercussions on the health of respective educational institutions. Those getting positioned as institutional heads after seeking someone's blessings in any form are under monetary or other obligations.

This sacrificing of merit-based discharge of responsibilities by the apex authority concerned is highly deplorable. Monetized corruption by anyone in academics debilitates the institutions that are already struggling in penury and the requisite facilities could not be made available for students and teachers alike.

Besides resorting to unfair practices, the weak credentials of institutional heads do not permit them to lead the academic community effectively and the governance becomes extreme authority-centric. The people who are good at academics usually may not speak against weak leadership but have no intellectual respect for such leadership which eventually results in their whole-hearted withdrawal from the institutional functioning.

Most of the time the fear psychosis of mediocre academic heads leads to their reliance on hypocrites and weak academic people and the quality of deliveries to the students gets affected severely. The loss of sound training opportunities to the younger teachers by senior teachers is also one of the prominent damages incurred due to it.

The impact of poor quality is felt by the vicious loop created by mediocrity thriving mediocrity in education. Thence the compromises made in engaging human resources in academic processes is the corruption that impacts the future and is unpardonable.

Weakening integrity of education processes

Question paper leakages, copying, plagiarism, biases in assessments, etc. are often observed to impact the integrity of education processes. The examination being an integral part of the education system, it's important to look at the vulnerable elements which start from paper setting, moderation, printing, distribution, conduction, evaluation, and ends at the result declaration. The breach of integrity at any stage questions the whole process.

It is seen that temptation to infringement of the hallowed processes to oblige preferred few based on financial or other gratifications. This develops trust deficit and frustration among the stakeholders. Ubiquitously the corruption is the driving potential behind violating the holy examination-evaluation system and the loss incurred is irreparable. The lust for money and misusing position of authority is pernicious for the education system as a whole.

Apart from disrupting the confidentiality of processes, partisanship by teaching fraternity is much more dangerous. The students perceiving any kind of bias in their qualitative evaluation by their teachers is exasperating and inculcates a propensity of exercising similar counter biases after attaining the positions of authority in the future. The occurrences of plagiarism by teachers and students show their predilection to taking shortcut routes and is very discomforting.

However, the University Grants Commission has promulgated the regulations for curbing these practices, but the germination of a tendency to copy questions the credibility of the concerned.

Corruption of any type in the education system ends up intoxicating future generations and is much more dreadful as compared to damage due to financial corruption in other sectors. The poor quality of education may not be prima-facie monetary corruption but the loss incurred by it through the inadequately educated youths will equate to an unbelievable amount of money while jeopardizing sustainability and hampering the growth of civilization. Time is ripe with ample pointers for the education regulators and government to ponder upon the issues emanating from the ongoing assault on the virtuousness of the education system lest the demographic dividend is lost.

****

CHAPTER XXVIII

Withering Public Sector and Bourgeoning Private Sector in Higher Education

The annual overall ranking of higher education institutions (HEIs) by the National Institutional Ranking Framework (NIRF) demonstrates burgeoning private sector institutions. Top 100 institutions in NIRF overall ranking list of HEIs in years 2019, 2020, and 2021 has around 27% – 30% institutions of the private sector. A closer look at the top 50 ranks points to a rise in the number of private-sector HEIs from 7 in 2019 & 2020 to 10 in 2021. In the university category rankings of 2020 and 2021, the private sector universities constitute more than 40% of the top 100 ranks. Similarly, in the category of engineering institutions ranking list of 2020 and 2021, the number of private-sector HEIs is more than 30% in the top 100 ranks. Flourishing private sector HEIs is a positive sign in overall higher education, nevertheless, the shrinking number of public sector HEIs in the top 100 ranks is concerning because of the inadequacy of quality output from the public sector HEIs established and run by taxpayers money.

All India Survey of Higher Education (AISHE) reports the presence of 31390 private colleges, 396 private universities, and 88 private Deemed-to-be universities out of a total of 1043 Universities, 42343 colleges, and 11779 standalone colleges in the country in the year 2020. Because of the affiliation of the colleges being with 307 universities of the public sector, the teaching-learning and allied processes in the colleges can be considered to be under the control of public sector universities. Thence, an honest introspection of critical limitations of public sector HEIs in delivering good performance is inevitable.

Prima facie comparison of scores of the topmost public sector institution and the highest-ranking private sector institution in different attributes prescribed by the overall NIRF ranking list shows that the private HEIs primarily lag in 'faculty qualification and experience', 'financial resources & their utilization', 'quality of research output in terms of number & quality of publications', 'intellectual patent rights & patents', 'projects & professional practices', 'catering to economically & socially challenged students', and 'perception ranking'.

Simultaneously, the shrinking number of public sector institutions in top ranks indicates their poor scores in 'teaching, learning & resources', 'research and professional practices', 'graduation outcomes', 'outreach and inclusivity' despite having good peer perception on account of being HEIs in government control. The attainments in these attributes are the culmination of the efficacy of governance, financing, processes, and practices that influence the quality of education, research, and outreach in HEIs. Therefore, the key for speedy amelioration of the quality of deliverables lies in improving critical enablers like governance, financing, human resource, and students in public sector HEIs.

For quite some time, the governance of higher education that revolves around its leader has been witnessing numerous controversies. With the conspicuous leadership in HEIs as per frequent news reports, the integrity of its selection process becomes contentious. On the face of it, the recent news of huge cash recovery during a raid on the premises of the Vice-Chancellor of Bihar University illustrates that all is not well. The arrest of Vice-Chancellors of Universities in Rajasthan, Tamil Nadu, on charges of taking bribes in the recent past decree the fragile integrity of academic leadership. Also, there are numerous reports of bribery in the process of appointment. Candid news reports about financial corruption, and the appointment of persons with questionable administrative and academic integrities as Vice-Chancellors / Directors in Universities / Institutions puts the whole process under the scanner. The apex positions being adorned by persons of poor integrity, values, and academic credentials push the institutional governance in shambles.

Academic leaders are purported to possess utmost integrity, commitment, moral and ethical values apart from requisite academic credentials to act as a role model in the institution. Unequivocally, the teaching community can not afford to be immoral, unethical, apathetic, and non-believer of merit in general. Any deviation will mar the quality of education in HEIs.

The obvious precondition for ensuring good performance from HEIs is the sacrosanct and merit-based process of picking up human resources as its leader, teachers, and staff. Unfortunately, the present circumstances speak of absence in fairness and disregard of merit & other attributes in the recruitment of human resources in public sector HEIs, resulting in such institutions becoming vulnerable to lose on performance indicators.

In public sector HEIs, primarily it is the lack of individual ownership and accountability of those at the helm, that germinates the possibility of malpractices. Secondly, the degeneration gets amplified by the vicious trap created due to the corruption breeds corruption. Thirdly, it is the procedural safeguards offering little immunity to individuals, job security, and public financing of wages that do not let them feel the pinch of incurring damage.

Contrary to it, the private sector HEIs have individual ownership, minimum checks, and balances for speedy execution of processes, quicker decision making, and the absence of an immunity to individuals except for the promoters. This entrusts them with an opportunity to excel. However, most private sector HEIs fail to unleash their strengths because of the latent intent of promoters to maximize return on investment. As a result, their lesser spending on human resources and inadequate up-gradation of teaching–research support systems constrains them to achieve excellence.

But, the blossoming of few private sector HEIs as evident from their good rankings and sizeable share among top ranking institutions establishes that self-financed institutions too can achieve excellence, provided there is a strong will. However, private sector HEIs need to focus on financial resource mobilization as its deficiency affects the quality of human resource and teaching-research infrastructure. Concerted efforts are required by the regulators of public sector HEIs to ensure fair, merit-centric, and transparent hiring of human resources at all levels through processes of impeccable integrity. Concurrently, the financial crunch faced by public sector HEIs calls for enhancing public investment in education to 6% of GDP as ordained by the Kothari Commission report and NEP 2020 both.

****

CHAPTER XXIX

Time to remodel technical education for Industry 5.0

A paradigm shift in the choices exercised by Generation Z is putting a labyrinthian challenge of the best brains opting for the computer science and associated disciplines of study only. This trend is seen since the last few years in admissions to engineering programmes in the country. The choices of engineering aspirants seem to be greatly influenced by the employment opportunities offered by the respective programme of study. This has resulted in the subjects catering to collaboration between human and artificial intelligence (AI) coming out in great demand. Symbiotic human-AI partnership for the smart factories of next-generation as envisaged in the Industry 4.0 seems to be pushing for it, nevertheless, the separation of core engineering domains from the newer computer-based technologies will never take place.

The use of high-end computational facilities, data storage and its retrieval, integration of information, communication, and artificial intelligence in systems will essentially call for robust core engineering fundamentals. That is why with the changing time, it is felt that the emphasis has to be shifted beyond merely producing goods and services for profit. Industry 5.0 underlines the fifth industrial revolution that will reduce focus on technology and enhance collaborations between humans and machines by dismantling the boundaries between various engineering disciplines. The ubiquitous application of drone technology, robotics, and artificial intelligence reiterates the changing industry vision. This human-robot collaboration termed 'cobots' contemplates the co-working of human and intelligent machines in industrial environments as well as in normal life. This preconditions the ample no. of trained personnel for the anticipated Industry 5.0 vision. Simultaneously, the digital twins is another fast-growing technological change that involves the visualisation of complex products and processes, their design, manufacturing, functioning, and maintenance through suitable software for human interactions with machines.

Undoubtedly, the huge digital interventions in existing processes and their remodelling are going to offer transformations in industrial practices and processes. Thence, the engineering systems have to be compatible with the cyber-physical interventions in them along with provisioning of the efficiently trained professionals to nurture effective outputs from them. The manner in which the manufacturing sector has to flourish under the changing productive and economic scenario in the future needs to be understood, else the existing companies will not be able to take competing advantages.

This calls for a proper balance between the modernisation of machines and human resources. As a result, the engineering curriculum may have to be cross-fertilised from the perspective of digital metamorphoses. However, the fundamentals are not going to change and the essence of the core curriculum of different disciplines of engineering and technology remains intact even with the digitalisation creeping into them.

The National Education Policy 2020 (NEP) has explicitly attempted for creating the requisite eco-system for making existing education programmes multidisciplinary. This is because of the need for a skilled workforce, particularly involving mathematics, computer science, and data science, in conjunction with multidisciplinary abilities across the sciences, social sciences, and humanities. The ensuing challenge for fulfilling worldwide requirements of energy, water, food, sanitation, etc. will necessitate virtuoso human resources to make inevitable intercessions and thus corroborate the remodelling of technical education.

It is noteworthy that the choice-based credit system (CBCS) was introduced in the country long back and paved the way for students to choose assorted subjects in every programme suiting their interests and passion. University Grants Commission has constantly impelled for CBCS, but the institutions, in general, could not implement the CBCS due to limitations of the availability of teachers and required infrastructure. Thus, the students were deprived of the opportunity of seeking multidisciplinary education and the educational programmes remained stereotyped as traditional. Had the choices of subjects focussing around the present jobs been exercised by students pursuing technical education programmes, the uneven employment scenario could have been taken care of to a certain extent.

Indisputably, the marginalisation of the manufacturing sector has pushed for the unprecedented rise of the service economy due to the dominance of the service sector consisting of trade, hotel, restaurants, transportation, storage, communication, financing, insurance, business services, community, social and personal services, construction services, etc. Besides, the growth of the manufacturing sector is ineluctable for the healthy economy, which in turn pegs at the adequately trained technical human resource as per synchronic sustainable development.

The apparent trends of Industry 4.0 moving on to Industry 5.0 entail alterations in the engineering curriculum to imbibe students with capabilities to support the use of cyber-physical systems in every domain of engineering and technology. The contemporary aspirations for improvising every process concerning its productivity obligates the annihilation of the existing rigid compartmentalisation of different programmes. The curriculum warrants inclusion of requisite courses that ingrain IT proficiencies along with core capabilities through provisions of major and minor subjects for enhancing abilities pertaining to varying specialisations. Brooding on the revision of the syllabus to meet the current aspirations from the technical professionals leads to embedding every subject with experiential learning through applications of the contents covered in it along with using IT tools to make the knowledge application much more proficient. Adding cyber-physical intrusions to various possible subjects in the curriculum will automatically change the flavour of the respective programmes to industry-friendly. This will gear up the engineers and technologists from every discipline to fit in the forthcoming upgrades due to cyber-physical initiatives and eventually end the lopsided drive to get trained in IT and computer-based disciplines.

Revamping the engineering curriculum for handling the revolutionary advances in businesses, industry practices, and innovations for better performance will hold the skewed exodus of brilliant minds to certain IT-centric engineering programmes. Inarguably, there is a need for brighter minds in every walk of life and the ongoing major requisition for only computer-trained manpower should not be misperceived as the reducing demand for the professionals from other core disciplines of engineering like civil, electrical, mechanical, chemical, etc. The sustainability of civilisation and its growth sanctions the education system to roll out knowledgeable, competent, and capable educated students. The contorted flow of sharper minds to certain disciplines of engineering and technology is concerning and impresses the regulators and government to ponder upon proper human resource planning and mandating the academics for enriching the knowledge base of technical professionals to fit in the vision of Industry 5.0.

****

References

1. 2020: A Year of Shambolic Education Burdening Learners,www.therise.co.in, *on 31st December 2020, https://therise.co.in/5864/a-year-of-shambolic-education-burdening-learners/*

2. Is upending teacher eligibility qualifications the panacea for higher education?, *www.ifp.co.in, on 2nd January 2021, https://www.ifp.co.in/opinion/is-upending-teacher-eligibility-qualifications-the-panacea-for-higher-education*

3. How to reach the milestones set in the new education policy framework, *www.ifp.co.in, on 30th January 2021, https://www.ifp.co.in/opinion/how-to-reach-the-milestones-set-in-the-new-education-policy-framework*

4. Another Sci-Tech Policy in the Offing!,*www.therise.co.in, on 31st January 2021, https://therise.co.in/6040/another-science-and-technology-policy-in-the-offing/*

5. Rhetoric of common syllabus in universities may diminish possibility of achieving excellence, *www.ifp.co.in, on 12th February 2021, https://www.ifp.co.in/opinion/rhetoric-of-common-syllabus-in-universities-may-diminish-possibility-of-achieving-excellence*

6. Outsourcing teachers: A new paradigm in higher education - Gurus Being Outsourced in 'Vishwaguru' India,*www.therise.co.in, on 08th March 2021, https://therise.co.in/6149/outsourcing-teachers-in-higher-education/*

7. How feasible is Engineering Education without Physics and Mathematics, *www.ifp.co.in, on 19th March 2021,https://www.ifp.co.in/opinion/how-feasible-is-engineering-education-without-physics-and-mathematics*

8. How institutions can evolve to overcome learning gaps in online education in time of COVID-19, *www.ifp.co.in, on 11th April 2021, https://www.ifp.co.in/opinion/how-institutions-can-evolve-to-overcome-learning-gaps-in-online-education-in-time-of-covid-19*

9. Disruptions call for remodeling examinations and evaluation strategies amid COVID-19, *www.ifp.co.in, on 29th April 2021, https://www.ifp.co.in/opinion/disruptions-call-for-remodeling-examinations-and-evaluation-strategies-amid-covid-19*

10. Losing sheen of Guru Devo Bhava: An Introspection,*www.therise.co.in, on 30th April 2021, https://therise.co.in/6816/loosing-sheen-of-gurus/*

11. Education in Times of COVID: Shun End of Course Final Examinations, *www.ifp.co.in, on 24th May 2021,https://www.ifp.co.in/education/education-in-times-of-covid-shun-end-of-course-final-examinations*

12. Calibrate education in Corona aftermath,*www.therise.co.in, on 01st June 2021, https://therise.co.in/7208/calibrate-education-in-corona-aftermath/*

13. Scrapping of class 12 exams calls for onerous responsibility of redrafting evaluation strategy, *www.ifp.co.in, on 02nd June 2021, https://www.ifp.co.in/analysis/scrapping-of-class-12-exams-calls-for-onerous-responsibility-of-redrafting-evaluation-strategy*

14. Exam Hesitancy: Drawbacks in e-learning seem to have shaken confidence of students for undertaking exams, *www.ifp.co.in, on 22nd June 2021, https://www.ifp.co.in/opinion/exam-hesitancy-drawbacks-in-e-learning-seem-to-have-shaken-confidence-of-students-for-undertaking-exams*

15. Blended Learning in Indian Higher Education: How Feasible is it?, *www.therise.co.in, on 30th June 2021,*

https://therise.co.in/7738/blended-learning-in-higher-education/

16. Remodelling of class 10, 12 assessment calls for utmost care, www.ifp.co.in, *on 09th July 2021,* https://www.ifp.co.in/analysis/remodelling-of-class-10-12-assessment-calls-for-utmost-care

17. Anniversary of NEP 2020: Education needs intensive care, www.therise.co.in,*on 29th July 2021,* https://therise.co.in/8175/anniversary-of-nep-2020/

18. Why students are steering away from engineering education in India?, www.ifp.co.in, *on 01st August 2021, https://www.ifp.co.in/analysis/why-students-are-steering-away-from-engineering-education-in-india*

19. Why India seeks higher education in public sector and school education in private sector?, www.ifp.co.in, *on 25th August 2021, https://www.ifp.co.in/analysis/why-india-seeks-higher-education-in -public-sector-and-school-education-in-private-sector*

20. Education system in vicious trap of insufficiency and amotivation of teachers in India, www.ifp.co.in, *on 12th September 2021, https://www.ifp.co.in/analysis/education-system-in-vicious-trap-of-insufficiency-and-amotivation-of-teachers-in-india*

21. The Great Indian Distressful Examinations: An Introspection, www.therise.co.in, *on 24th September 2021,* https://therise.co.in/8944/indian-distressful-examinations-introspection/

22. Test Culture in India: Boon or Bane, www.ifp.co.in, *on 09th October 2021, https://www.ifp.co.in/education/test-culture-in-india-boon-or-bane*

23. Equitable and Accessible Education in COVID-hit India: A Mirage?, www.therise.co.in, *on 21st October 2021,* https://therise.co.in/9168/

supreme-court-on-access-to-education/

24. Dissecting selection of leadership in higher education institutions, www.ifp.co.in, *on 26th October 2021, https://www.ifp.co.in/opinion/ dissecting-selection-of-leadership-in-higher-education-institutions*

25. Metamorphosing Industry 4.0 to Industry 5.0 Requires Engineers From All Domains, www.therise.co.in, *on 15th November 2021, https://therise.co.in/9461/ metamorphosing-industry-requires-all-engineers/*

26. Money matters in Higher Education, www.ifp.co.in, *on 03rd December 2021, https://www.ifp.co.in/opinion/ money-matters-in-higher-education*

27. Corruption breeds corruption and education is no exception, www.timesofindia.indiatimes.com, *on 09th December 2021, https://timesofindia.indiatimes.com/blogs/ onkar-singh/ corruption-breeds-corruption-and-education-is-no-exception/*

28. Withering Public Sector and Bourgeoning Private Sector in Higher Education, www.therise.co.in, *on 12th December 2021, https://therise.co.in/9688/ higher-education-in-public-private-sector/*

29. Time to remodel technical education for Industry 5.0, www.ifp.co.in, *on 16th December 2021, https://www.ifp.co.in/opinion/ time-to-remodel-technical-education-for-industry-50*

Printed by Libri Plureos GmbH in Hamburg, Germany